>

Institution of Civil Engineers

D1471097

CLIENT BEST
PRACTICE GUIDE

Editors: Sue Kershaw and David Hutchison

**Published for the Institution of Civil Engineers
by Thomas Telford Limited,**
40 Marsh Wall, London E14 9TP, UK.
www.thomastelford.com

Distributors for Thomas Telford books are
USA: ASCE Press, 1801 Alexander Bell Drive,
Reston, VA 20191-4400, USA
Australia: DA Books and Journals,
648 Whitehorse Road, Mitcham 3132, Victoria

First published 2009
A catalogue record for this book is available from the British Library
ISBN: 978-0-7277 3650-5

Designed by Kneath Associates, Swansea
Printed and bound in Great Britain by
Latimer Trend & Company Ltd., Plymouth

Contents

>

Foreword

During my career both as a civil engineer and a parliamentarian, I have always realised the importance of construction clients – and the impact and influence they can bring to delivering society's building and infrastructure successfully.

Yet there is very little available to inform construction clients on best practice and help them lead their projects. As a result there is an increased risk of projects running late, over budget or failing to deliver their intended benefits.

This *Client Best Practice Guide* fills the gap, a slim compendium of advice compiled by experienced professionals with pan-industry input. It is a shining example of the genuinely good and independent guidance that can be produced by the learned society of the Institution of Civil Engineers.

Rt Hon Nick Raynsford
MP

Preface

It has been my great honour and privilege to Chair the Expert Panel set up by the Learned Society of the Institution of Civil Engineers to produce this guide. The concept of the guide was first raised in March 2008, and has been developed by the panel which represents all facets of the Institution's membership and, collectively, many years of experience in the construction industry. The intention of the guide is to be a one-stop ready reference and route map for achieving best practice from a construction client's perspective – regardless of sector or scale.

It is not intended to be a textbook, a research report or a comprehensive tome of facts and methodologies; rather it is an encapsulation, in the words of Dr Martin Barnes CBE, of 'the best way we do things now'.

Drawing on existing best practice and an excellent source of data collected through one-to-one interviews with industry leaders, it can be used by clients, all project professionals and ICE members to sample, champion – and challenge – what is perceived as best practice, and signpost where more information can be found.

This is only the beginning of this initiative to disseminate best practice in construction and it will be developed further by the learned society to meet the needs of the industry.

Sue Kershaw
Head of Programme Management,
ODA Transport, Olympic Delivery Authority

Acknowledgements

ICE Client Best Practice Panel

Chair and Editor: Sue Kershaw, *Olympic Delivery Authority*

Editor: David Hutchison, *Parsons Brinckerhoff*

Peter Cunningham, *Constructing Excellence*

Darren Dobson, *Costain*

Tony Francis, *Department for Transport*

Ian Gardner, *Arup*

Blessing Gwena, *Kier Group*

Peter Hansford, *The Nichols Group*

Leon Heward-Mills, *Thomas Telford*

Michael Jones, *Trimentis*

Peter McDermott, *University of Salford*

Mike Napier, *Costain*

Nelson Ogunshakin, *Association for Consultancy and Engineering*

Alasdair Reisner, *Civil Engineering Contractors Association*

Steering group

Tim Chapman, *Arup*

Charly Clark, *Costain*

Andy Gooding, *Institution of Civil Engineers*

Secretariat

Salima Hernandez, *Institution of Civil Engineers*

Advisory group

Martin Barnes, *MPA and APM*

Graham Dalton, *The Highways Agency*

John Hawkins, *Institution of Civil Engineers*

John Lofty, *JJL Consultancy Ltd*

Mike Nichols, *The Nichols Group*

Tony Ridley, *Imperial College*

Steve Rowsell, *CrossRail*

Consultees

Mark Adams, John Armitt, Charles Ball, Martin Barnes, Rosemary Beales, David Brewer, Nigel Brown, Richard Butterfield, Sharni Clark, Hugh Coakley, Graham Dalton, Peter Davis, Andrew Elliott, Nick Field, Julian Garrett, David Gavaghan, Alistair Godbold, Tim Grimshaw, Roger Hawkins, David Higgins, Keith Howells, John Ioannou, Philip Isgar, Steve Jessop, Steve Jones, Norman Kerfoot, Nirmal Kotecha, Martin Land, Maggie Latham, Nick Lawton, Nick Layton, Quentin Leiper, John Lofty, Adrian Malone, Bill McElroy, Paul McLarnon, Andrew McNaughton, Sir Adrian Montague, Jerry Morrisey, Jon Neale, Mike Nichols, Martin Nielsen, Malcolm Noyce, Mark Richardson, Tony Ridley, Sally Roe, Martin Rowark, Steve Rowsell, Ian Simms, Mike Sinclair-Williams, David Staniforth, James Stewart, Hugh Sumner, David Suratgar, Andrew Thomas, David Toolan, Sanjay Trivedi, Derek Turner, Geoff Virrels, Richard Walker, Sir Robert Walmsley, Roy Westbrook, Duncan Whiting, George Wilton, Clive Winkler, Gary Wright, David Yeoell.

Endorsements

"I welcome this guide wholeheartedly, both as a major public sector client and an advisor to the panel. It provides clear advice and highlights best practice, which, if acted on, will raise the standard of 'clienting'."

Graham Dalton,
Chief Executive, The Highways Agency

"I am pleased that this guidance has been published. It is in everyone's interests to ensure that projects are delivered on time, on budget and to the highest standards, and ACE members are at the forefront of delivering high quality professional services. However, clients also have a vital role to play in ensuring best practice is put into operation. The principles set out here can be applied to practically every civil engineering and construction project anywhere in the world. I am confident that, if this guidance is put into practice, clients, consultants and the entire supply chain will work together more effectively – to the benefit of everyone."

Nelson Ogunshakin,
Chief Executive, Association for Consultancy and Engineering

consultancy **engineering** business **environment**

"My career has been centred on advising clients on how their projects can be delivered efficiently, effectively, and provide good value for money. This guide, the first of its kind, provides the same sort of pragmatic advice, and signposts where further help can be found. I recommend it as a good read for both clients and suppliers alike."

Mike Nichols,
Chairman and Chief Executive, The Nichols Group

"There are many examples of good practice that can be found in client organisations throughout the construction sector as clients work to improve themselves, their supply chains and the projects they deliver. Yet all too often this best practice remains rooted within those organisations. The authors of this guide are to be commended for producing a document which shares so many of these ideas and which has the potential to benefit the whole industry."

Rosemary Beales,
National Director, Civil Engineering Contractors Association

"The Construction Clients' Group welcomes this Guide as it includes many of the critical ingredients that enable clients to get better value from their construction procurement. We have enjoyed contributing to the Guide and advocating best practice through better integration of the supply chain combined with collaborative working principles. We hope that this Guide and the associated diagnostic tool inspires the reader to take a different approach to their client role within the construction supply chain and enable them to proactively engage with our industry in delivering a better built environment."

Peter Cunningham,
Chief Executive, Construction Clients' Group

Introduction

The aim of this guide

The role and performance of clients is the single most important factor in determining the success of construction projects and capital works programmes, regardless of their size, complexity or location.

There are plenty of guides on how to be a good project manager but nothing on the market explaining to clients the many ways in which they can positively influence the success of their projects – both during the planning, development and implementation stages as well as during operation and final decommissioning.

The Institution of Civil Engineers (ICE) has thus embarked on a major initiative to identify best practice in UK construction project procurement and delivery, and to share it as widely among client organisations and its members as possible.

Fortunately there are many examples of good client practice in the UK construction industry, as well as many organisations promoting best practice. The purpose of this unique guide is to bring these initiatives together under one banner and share their outputs across the industry for everyone's benefit.

Specifically, the guide aims to furnish UK construction clients with the information they need to answer the following questions.

> Am I using best practice?

> How can this be assessed?

> How does this lead to project success?

It is a high-level document, providing an overview of the way clients should be approaching the planning, development, implementation, operation and decommissioning of their projects. It is intended primarily for UK clients of infrastructure projects large and small, but is equally applicable to all public and private sector construction clients and their advisors worldwide.

How to use the guide

Each of the guide's chapters focuses on specific issues that clients need to consider, and identify aspects of client performance that will help achieve a successful project outcome. They examine various aspects of clients' input and provide guidance on measures that have been found to be particularly influential. Sources of referenced publications and websites are provided in each chapter, alongside lists of further reading for those wishing to undertake more detailed study.

Ideally this document should be read in its entirety before any work starts, giving clients an independent overview of best practice before they start working within any pre-established approaches for their organisation or sector. However, clients and others already involved in construction projects will find that the guide and its individual chapters serve as useful road maps, regardless of what aspect or stage of a project they are currently in.

How the guide was developed

The expert panel set up by ICE to produce this guide has consulted widely. It has drawn on existing practice and an excellent source of data collected through one-to-one interviews with industry leaders. A small advisory panel consisting of very senior members of the profession was consulted on the first and final drafts of the guide and the concept was discussed with the Major Projects Association (MPA) Board and at special meetings held with members of the MPA. NETLIPSE (Network for the dissemination of knowledge on the management and organisation of Large Infrastructure Projects in Europe – an EU-sponsored research project) was also consulted together with the NEC users group. The expert panel also sent questionnaires to over 40 000 of the ICE's members, who between them form a significant sounding board of clients and those who work for clients in construction. The feedback reinforced the need for the guide.

The ClientMAP online assessment tool

It is proposed that the guide will foster a whole suite of sub-documents to supplement the many important areas and practices that are no more than outlined here. The first step in this process is the development of an online assessment tool to help clients see where they are in terms of using best practice – see page 35 for further details.

The Client best practise guide's online maturity assessment profile tool (ClientMAP) is designed to help clients who have read this guide go on to assess where they are in terms of using best practice.

Being online it will enhance the capability of the tool for scoring and presenting results compared to a strictly paper-based version. It also allows for future developments, for example as a body of knowledge which will build through use – comparative results will be provided to users. Eventually the assessment will form part of a structured benchmarking process, potentially involving independent assessments.

This Guide, together with the associated best practice assessment tool, will help clients deliver successful projects. This will in turn raise the profile positively of the whole construction sector and create lasting legacies of which we can all be proud.

David Hutchison,
ICE Vice President and Principal Consultant,
Rail, Parsons Brinckerhoff

1. What makes a successful client?

Contents

> *'A successful project requires clear client vision – clear about what they want and articulated well.'*
> Richard Butterfield, Project manager

The role

The client is the organisational entity or individual within the public or private sector organisation that commissions the project. It is considered to be of great advantage when the client is a named individual who is accountable for the benefits of that project which might be functional, financial, environmental, societal or reputational.

The client 'owns' the business case of a project on behalf of the client organisation. Key to this is for there to be no ambiguity in who is acting in the client role. It is important for the client to understand what decisions are required when. The client should provide effective leadership of the project, which should start at the strategic level within the client organisation (ref Construction Clients' Group, 2008) but which should permeate all levels. This includes creating and communicating a vision for the project that will enable the business and all other participants to understand its purpose.

The principal role of clients is to ensure that they achieve a solution to their business goals and to do this they have to:

> apply effective leadership and governance

> create the project environment for success

> create interdependent roles

> provide relationship management (internally and externally)

> provide strategic thinking, intent and approach and

> set priorities.

It should also be recognised that, while the project will have an ultimate client, there may be several individuals acting for supply chain companies who will also be fulfilling this role for their part of the project if they themselves employ sub-consultants or subcontractors.

Characteristics of a good client

There is a number of characteristics that define a good client for a construction project. These include:

> having a strong belief in and commitment to the project

> being driven by results and committed to success

> holding a deep concern for people, supporting and enthusing them

> generating trust, respect and appropriate behaviours within the team.

Good clients have a wide breadth of view, and are frequently networking and lobbying. They are thinkers, exploring and challenging issues and angles. They demonstrate courage, taking calculated risks, and show flexibility, adjusting their approach as

Figure 1.1. Successful projects have clients with strong belief and commitment

Image courtesy of Troika/LCR

necessary. Good clients are not concerned with their personal status. And, crucially, they are good managers of time: both their own and that of others.

Eight key tasks

The role of project clients is multi-faceted and complex. However, in essence, they should focus on eight key tasks.

1 Strategy – owning and maintaining the strategy for a project.

2 Project environment – creating the right project environment and carefully monitoring it, staying vigilant for changes that might impact on a project and its business.

3 Business case – establishing a clear business case at the outset of a project, and then constantly revisiting it, verifying its assumptions, objectives and its ongoing validity.

4 High-level progress – focusing more on prognosis rather than monitoring detailed progress.

5 Corrective action – taking clear and timely decisions throughout the design and construction process; being ready to 'press the start button' if corrective action is required; similarly, being prepared to 'press the stop button' if a project becomes unviable.

6 Communication – communicating widely: to the client organisation, the project team and those affected by the project.

7 Stakeholders – seeking to understand and, where possible, satisfy the requirements of all parties with an interest or concern in a project.

8 Lessons – learning from other projects and from working closely with other clients, both within the organisation and in the wider industry.

'While it is entirely possible that changes in the client's requirements over the life of the project may lead to amendments of the original brief, the project will benefit from setting a clear description of what is going to be delivered at an early stage, providing confidence to the whole project team.'
Construction industry specialist

Relationship with other key roles

Clients have a number of key relationships to achieve a successful project outcome (ref Office of Government Commerce, 2007a). These are with:

> the project manager – who can be part of the client team or the supply team, and who delivers the development and implementation of the project (see Chapters 4 and 5)

> technical advisors – those organisations who provide advice on financing, planning, architecture, compliance with regulations and who shape the project in its initial stages. They are integral in formulating the client's requirements

> the design team – those who integrate client's requirements into workable solutions and involve engineers, architects and other supporting disciplines.

> the supply team – the interlinked group of contractors and manufacturers that provides the various elements of the work, the input of which is managed by the project manager (see Chapter 5)

> the operator, or customer – to take over and operate the new asset and realise the benefits (see Chapter 8).

The client, project manager, supply chain and operator need to work as an effective 'project team' for successful achievement of

2   //   Client best practice guide

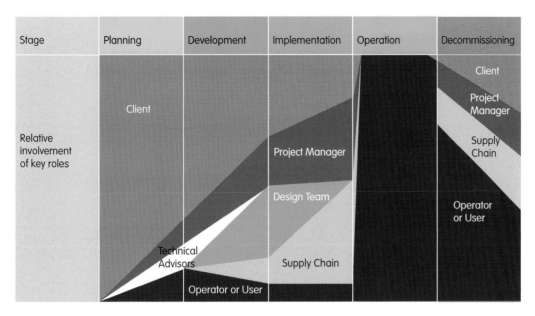

| Stage | Planning | Development | Implementation | Operation | Decommissioning |

Figure 1.2. The client's role should continue throughout a project's lifecycle to ensure success (after Martin Barnes)

a project (ref Major Projects Association, 2001; Strategic Forum for Construction, 2003, 2007; Office of Government Commerce, 2007b; Construction Clients' Group and Business Vantage, 2009).

Role over life of project

Clients play a vital role at every stage of a project's lifecycle (see Chapter 2): from initial inception through planning, development, implementation up to entry into operation. Similarly, clients have a key role to play during decommissioning. The intensity of the role changes over the lifecycle, with some stages requiring much greater input than others, but nevertheless clients have a distinct role to play throughout (see Figure 1.2).

Leadership of a project

Effective leadership requires demonstrable personal commitment, typically described as 'this is someone I want to follow'.

Major projects develop their own unique culture – 'the way we will do things around here' – and this stems from the client. A key element of culture is behaviour, and the behaviour of clients and their senior team will be closely watched by the supply team. Clients thus have a key influence on behaviour within the whole project team.

Setting the priorities

Many people involved with projects are familiar with the time–cost–performance triangle (Figure 1.3). This illustrates the sometimes difficult trade-offs that have to be made between these three primary variables. Clients should define at the outset the priorities for a project in relation to these three variables (ref Saxon, 2005) particularly in relationship to their business, customer and operational priorities.

For example, for major event facilities, while cost and performance cannot be flexed with ease, time is paramount. On the other hand, performance might be of greater importance than time and cost on a research and development project.

In addition to time, cost and performance, there are many other considerations for clients, such as sustainability, environmental, health and safety, public policy, equality and diversity, access and inclusion (see Chapter 6). Nevertheless, a careful assessment of where a project needs to aim within the time–cost–performance triangle will provide a crucial direction to the project team and inform decisions when hard choices have to be made. In this way clients are able to steer a project through the complexity of decision making, with a clear focus on its purpose and priorities.

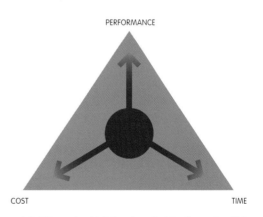

Figure 1.3. Clients should define the priorities for trade-offs between time, cost and performance from the beginning of a project

'If the governance is not clear from the outset, this will affect supplier confidence in the client as an organisation, and their bid will reflect this. Just as clients may ask suppliers to demonstrate that key staff are committed to the project, the client organisation itself should be able to show that it has committed suitable staff to the project in order to build confidence.' Rosemary Beales, Civil Engineering Contractors Association

Governance

The term 'governance' is used to describe the way in which a project is authorised, conducted and overseen by the client organisation and significant interested parties, such as sponsors, funders and regulators. It is a mechanism for engaging the client organisation in a project, for securing buy-in of key players and for driving executive decision making. The governance process includes establishing appropriate and effective delegations of responsibility.

There is no 'one size fits all' governance structure; project governance needs to be appropriate to a particular project and client organisation. Clients typically establish a 'project board' to fulfil the governance function. Where an organisation carries out multiple projects, a 'programme board' or 'portfolio board' might be established, with project boards reporting to it.

It is essential that the client, project manager and operator all attend the project board, preferably as full members. Other parties might be represented on the board, particularly if they have a funding or equity stake in a project or if their involvement is vital to a project's success. It is normal practice for the client to chair the project board.

Research has shown that a governance process is at its most effective when all interested parties are actively involved and can communicate constructively in an open environment.

'There is nothing worse than going to a designated person only to find that they do not have the power to act. There is a need to identify who the key people are in project governance at the outset of a project.' Construction industry specialist

Summary

> Clients are committed to success, are open-minded and good managers of people, risk and time.

> Clients lead the project team throughout a project's lifecycle to ensure successful delivery.

> In addition to setting the priorities between time, cost and quality, clients focus on strategy, the project environment, the business case, high-level progress, corrective action, communication, managing stakeholders and learning lessons.

> Clients need to establish a good governance structure, in which responsibility is delegated effectively.

References

1. Construction Clients' Group. *Client's Commitments Best Practice Guide,* Chapter 3 Client leadership, Constructing Excellence, London, November 2008. www.constructingexcellence.org.uk/sectorforums/constructionclientsgroup/clientcommitments/3.%20CL.pdf

2. Construction Clients' Group and Business Vantage. *Equal Partners – Customer and Supplier Alignment in Private Sector Construction,* Business Vantage, Windsor, January 2009. www.constructingexcellence.org.uk/sectorforums/constructionclientsgroup/reports/EP5.pdf

3. Major Projects Association. *Effective Teams for Complex Projects,* 2001. www.majorprojects.org/pubdoc/670.pdf

4. Office Of Government Commerce. Project Organisation – Roles and Responsibilities, CP0062, OGC, London, 2007a. www.ogc.gov.uk/documents/CP0062AEGuide2.pdf

5. Office Of Government Commerce. The Integrated Project Team – Teamworking and Partnering, CP0065, OGC, London, 2007b. www.ogc.gov.uk/documents/CP0065AEGuide5.pdf

6. SAXON, R. *Be Valuable: A guide to creating value in the built environment,* Constructing Excellence, London, November 2005. www.saxoncbe.com/bevaluable.pdf

7. Strategic Forum For Construction. *Integration Toolkit,* 2003. www.strategicforum.org.uk/sfctoolkit2/home/home.html

8. Strategic Forum For Construction. *Profiting from Integration,* Construction Industry Council, London, November 2007. www.strategicforum.org.uk/pdf/ITGReport120308.pdf

Further reading

> Aritua, Male, Bower. Defining the intelligent public sector construction client, *Management, Procurement and Law,* 01/05/2009.

> Buttrick R. *The Role of the Executive Project Sponsor,* Financial Times Prentice Hall, Harlow, 2003.

> Egan J. *Rethinking Construction,* Construction Task Force, November 1988.

> Fryer S. How to achieve true quality in construction, *Management, Procurement and Law,* 2007, **16,** No. 1.

> Hall M., Holt R. and Purchase D. Project sponsors under New Public Management: lessons from the frontline, *International Journal of Project Management,* 2003, **21.**

> Hamilton A. Managing projects: the role of a project support office, *Municipal Engineer,* 2006, **159,** Issue 3.

> Keeling D. Channel Tunnel Rail Link: quality management, *Civil Engineering,* 2003, **156,** Issue 5.

> Latham M. *Constructing the Team,* Department of It's Environment, London, 1994.

> Moorhouse Consulting, Benchmarking Programme Sponsors' Attitudes, *SRO Survey Results,* March/April 2009. www.morehouseconsultancy.com/knowledge/SRO-Survey1

> Platts J. and Tomasevic V. Developing productive relationships in civil engineering, *Civil Engineering,* 2006, **159,** Issue 3.

> Preston R. and Pugh D. *Seeking the Unicorn: The Research-based Pursuit of Sponsors and Sponsorship,* The Nichols Group, London, 2003.

> Project Management Institute. *A Guide to the Project Management Body of Knowledge (PMBOK®)* (3rd ed.), Project Management Institute, Newtown Square, PA, 2004.

> Royer I. Why bad projects are so hard to kill, *Harvard Business Review,* 2003, **81,** No. 2, 48–56.

> Thomsett R. Getting the Sponsor You Need, 2000. www.thomsett.com.au/main/articles/sponsor/toc.htm

2.Essential stages of a project

Contents

> *'Time spent during planning and development is far cheaper than fixing problems or changing direction during implementation, operation or decommissioning.'*
> Ian Gardner, Arup, Client consultant

The five stages

Experienced clients recognise that their projects go through a number of phases or work stages. These are structured to enable the viability of a project to be tested and for it to be monitored and controlled as it progresses.

The structure provides a 'project lifecycle' and helps to identify which key decisions and activities are required at which stage. Clients need to understand their inputs to their projects in the context of this lifecycle.

Clients of the most successful projects recognise and assess all of the following five stages when strategically considering their projects:

> *planning* – investment strategy, management strategy

> *development* – design development, procurement strategy, pre-construction

> *implementation* – detailed design, construction, commissioning

> *operation* – use, maintenance

> *decommissioning* – conversion, removal.

The subsequent chapters of this guide provide advice to clients through these five stages of the project lifecycle, focusing on what activities need to be considered and when.

Commonly used work-stage methodologies

The importance of having planned work stages through to project completion is recognised by many leading organisations in construction, including:

> Royal Institute of British Architects (RIBA): 'plan of work stages' A–L (ref RIBA, 2001)

> Office of Government Commerce (OGC): 'gateway approvals' 1–5 (ref Office of Government Commerce, 2007, Office of Government Commerce Gateway Process, 2009)

> Network Rail (NWR): 'guide to railway investment projects (GRIP) stages' 1–8 (ref Network Rail, 2007).

As can be seen from Figure 2.1, all three organisations recognise the importance of planning and development stages prior to implementation. OGC and NWR in particular consider the strategic need to establish a business case and output definition respectively, thus defining what functionality and performance will represent success. However, it should be noted that none of them has a stage gate for decommissioning.

Clients should consider their own particular objectives and determine how they want to prioritise work stages depending on the degree to which they have pre-established approaches for funding and management of their projects. The amount of emphasis to be placed on the planning and development stages will also be influenced by the degree to which the client's procurement strategy sets design as an up-front client-led activity or as a subset of a supplier-led design-and-build approach (see Chapter 5).

Experience suggests that the planning and development period is the most valuable in achieving a successful project outcome; helping clients to define what they really want, what they can afford and with what risk.

	PLANNING			DEVELOPMENT					IMPLEMENTATION		OPERATION
RIBA	**Stage A** Appraisal	**Stage B** Strategic Brief	**Stage C** Outline Proposals	**Stage D** Detailed Proposals	**Stage E** Final Proposals	**Stage F** Production Information	**Stage G** Tender Docs	**Stage H** Tender Action	**Stage J** Mobilsation	**Stage K** Construction to Practical Completion	**Stage L** After Practical Completion
OGC	**Gate 1** Business Justification			**Gate 2** Delivery Strategy		**Gate 3** Investment Decision			**Gate 4** Readiness for Service		**Gate 5** Operational Review and Benefits realisation
Network Rail	**GRIP 1** Output Definition	**GRIP 2** Prefessibilty	**GRIP 3** Option Selection	**GRIP 4** Single Option Selection		**GRIP 5** Detailed Design			**GRIP 6** Construction Test and Commission		**GRIP 7** Scheme Has Back / **GRIP 8** Project Close Out

Figure 2.1. The work stages, RIBA, OGC and NWR

Some specific areas where experienced clients recognise their input and direction can pay dividends as early as possible and throughout are:

> Consents and approvals – these can be often be protracted and involve participation from not only planning authorities but also many other major stakeholders such as the Environment Agency, English Heritage, Statutory Undertakers, the emergency services, etc. Having an excellent stakeholder management plan and communication plan can assist tremendously in this area. It is often the case that a Code of Construction Practice will also be required.

> Ground conditions – the ground is a frequent source of unwelcome surprises, as even in a good site investigation close to 100% of the soil remains uninvestigated. Typical problems involve the discovery of ground or groundwater contamination, valuable archaeology, unexpected buried services, large obstructions, geological features, flood risk or unstable ground. A thorough desk study to detect site-specific hazards is an essential investment.

> Waterproofing – a common disappointment is when water penetrates as it can significantly inhibit use of the final building, both through the building envelope above ground and through the substructure. Although often conservative solutions are adopted, they can turn out not to be conservative enough, and responsibility is often not clear, both through the design team and between design and construction.

> Traffic management – the amount of time and effort to gain approvals for this should not be underestimated. This will include traffic modelling and applying for Temporary and Permanent Traffic Regulation Orders.

It should also be recognised that the expenditure profile is usually at its peak during the implementation stage. Any delay to review and clarify objectives is much less costly to clients during the planning and development stages than during peak periods of construction or operation (see Figure 2.2).

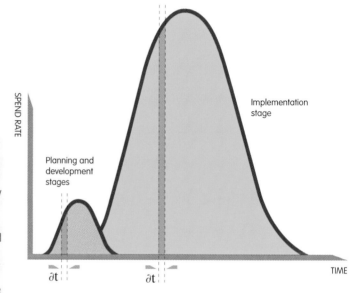

Figure 2.2. The costs of the same time delay are significantly greater during the implementation stage than during the planning and development stages

> 'In our experience, a project's success is often largely determined by the activities prior to implementation. To put it simply: plan long, build fast.'
> Phil Brand, Arup, Project manager

From cradle to grave

There is a tendency for projects to be focused on achieving project completion at the end of the implementation stage. Expressions such as 'delivered on time and on budget' are used to define successful projects at the end of this stage. Indeed, many of the work-stage models are set up to define the phases and activities needed to reach this point.

However, the best clients recognise that the success of a project is not defined by its implementation alone but by whether it meets and delivers the required functionality and performance within an overall investment cycle of capital and operational expenditure.

In addition to the initial planning, development and implementation stages, it is vital to consider operation from the outset. This may be recognised as the concept of 'use', but often there is a tendency in work-stage methodologies for the emphasis to be purely on getting a project into use rather than on whether it goes on to deliver against strategic intent.

Finally, the increasing importance that society is rightly placing on legacy and sustainability issues adds a further strategic consideration for clients. At the end of a construction project's useful life it needs to be possible to decommission it effectively, such that there is no long-term negative legacy imposed on future generations. To be able to satisfy this responsibly, a decommissioning stage also needs to be anticipated and planned for.

Summary

> Clients should consider all five lifecycle stages of a project to ensure a successful return on their total investment. These stages are planning, development, implementation, operation and decommissioning.

> Extra time spent during the planning and development stages is far cheaper than resolving problems or changing direction during the subsequent stages of implementation, operation and decommissioning.

References

1. Network Rail. *Guide to Railway Investment Projects* (GRIP), 2007. www.networkrail.co.uk/aspx/4171.aspx

2. Office of Government Commerce. Project Procurement Lifecycle – the Integrated Process, CP0063, OGC, London, 2007. www.ogc.gov.uk/documents/CP0063AEGuide3.pdf

3. Office of Government Commerce. *Gateway Process,* 2009. www.ogc.gov.uk/what_is_ogc_gateway_review.asp

4. Royal Institute of British Architects. *Plan of Work,* 2001. www.pedr.co.uk/textpage.asp?menu=1a&sortorder=130&area=main

Further reading

> Allport R. Operating risk: the Achilles' heel of major infrastructure projects, *Civil Engineering,* 2005, **158** Issue 3.

> ARYA C. and VASSIE P. R. Whole life cost analysis in concrete bridge tender evaluation, *Bridge Engineering,* 01/03/2004, **157**, Issue 1.

> Cooper, Stubbs, Carter, Dunn. Gibraltar runoff: a steep challenge for decommissioning, *Civil Engineering,* 01/02/2008, **161**, Issue 1.

> Gardner, Cruise, Sok, Krishnan, Dos Santos. Life-cycle costing of metallic structures, *Engineering Sustainability,* 01/12/2007, **160**, Issue 4.

> Hamilton A. Project start-up phase: the weakest link, *Municipal Engineer,* 01/12/2003, **156**, Issue 4.

> Menzies, Turan, Banfill. Life-cycle assessment and embodied energy: a review, *Construction Materials,* 01/11/2007, **160**, Issue 4.

3.Developing a delivery strategy

Contents

Developing the business case

Clients of successful construction projects have a clear vision and delivery strategy from the outset.

Clients need to identify the business requirements that a proposed project will fulfil and determine how the project sits within their overall business strategy. A clear vision for a project, which states the objectives and outcomes, is critical in justifying it in terms of investment and building the business case (ref Construction Clients' Group, 2008a).

Over 75% of people consulted in the preparation of this guide thought that having a clear description of strategic intent was essential to the success of their projects and all gave it a high degree of importance. Projects succeed as a consequence of a client embarking on a project having considered these matters rigorously and having described their strategic intent unambiguously.

The objectives and outcomes should be tested as the project progresses to check that it is still on track and that assumptions made in the business case remain valid. The gateway reviews, which some clients use to check the status of their projects at different stages of their maturity (see Chapter 2), provide the opportunity to verify and validate that a project still meets the requirements of the business case.

The reviews should be used to ensure that the strategic intent and objectives are still being followed and are still valid. A method known as 'systems engineering' can assist greatly with this approach and is becoming more widely used by clients. This is discussed in more detail later in this chapter.

Budget and best value

Clients should ensure that the budget provided in the business case is realistic and delivers best value. They should use 'whole-life costing', which involves considering planning, development, implementation, operation and decommissioning costs from the outset (ref Office of Government Commerce, 2007a; Saxon, 2005).

Sustainability and health and safety aspects should also be considered for a project as a whole (see Chapter 6). Value engineering is a tool which should be considered throughout a project to ensure that the most economically advantageous methods and materials are used and that the appropriate quality is being maintained.

Programme

Clients should also set a realistic and reasonable programme in the business case, which is likely to be attractive to the market place and attract competitive prices. The programme should identify all interdependencies as soon as possible so that the effects (e.g. delay or acceleration) can be identified immediately.

Risk management

Clients should work on understanding risks, how to handle risks (including their impact on relationships) and their attitude and appetite for them before considering risk allocation, risk management and risk registers (ref Office of Government Commerce, 2007b). Clients' insurers will also have a role in this aspect of a project.

Clients should operate a 'live' risk management process which, in larger organisations, is facilitated by risk managers.

Clients should include a project risk register in the business case from an early stage and use it throughout the life of a project. It is widely accepted that effective risk management assists a business to achieve its objectives by:

> reducing the likelihood or consequence of negative events

> identifying opportunities that would have a positive consequence

> identifying and understanding complex multiple cross-organisational risks

> supporting cost control

> developing best value through optioneering

> providing visible and auditable governance across all levels of an organisation

> protecting reputation and stakeholder confidence.

Clients should strive to develop their processes and experience in risk management – as illustrated in Figure 3.1.

Strategic Risk: A Guide for Directors (ref Actuarial Profession and Institution of Civil Engineers, 2006), compiled by a group of industry experts working under the auspices of the UK government, the Institution of Civil Engineers and the actuarial profession, provides a recommended approach to the management of strategic risk.

The Client Brief

The Client Brief should define what the client needs the project to achieve in order to deliver the success and values identified by the client's vision for the project. The Client Brief should also be anchored by the business case and should set objectives that are clearly within the envelope justified by the business case.

There can be different approaches in formulating the Client Brief. In some cases clients may have business-related or functional performance-related objectives and they may be open to how these may be realised. It is sometimes seen as an advantage to leave as much as possible open to allow creative or innovative

solutions to be developed from those with skills or experience that clients do not possess. In such cases a 'performance specification' approach should be taken.

In other cases clients may have a clear vision of how they see the project manifesting itself. They may already have completed similar projects and want many of the features of these incorporated. Then it may be more appropriate for a 'detailed design' to be prepared.

Systems engineering approach

Some clients are increasingly looking to systems engineering to deliver their projects (ref International Organization of Standardization, 2002 International Council on Systems Engineering, 2007; Woodcock, 2009). This approach considers both the business and technical needs of clients with the aim of providing a quality system that meets their goals.

The systems engineering approach is comprehensive and structured. It enables project teams to develop appropriate integrated solutions for the project that can be implemented as processes, products or services supported throughout a project's lifecycle to the satisfaction of everyone involved.

Figure 3.2 shows a systems engineering lifecycle or 'V-lifecycle' of a project. The diagram demonstrates the rigorous verification and validation checking at different stages of the project's lifecycle, from the project development stages through to the implementation and operation stages.

Projects often have many parties involved, either as contributors to the planning, development and implementation stages or as operators, maintainers and eventual decommissioners. The way in which data and information are assembled and used is therefore an important aspect of controlling the project outcome and whether it is successful.

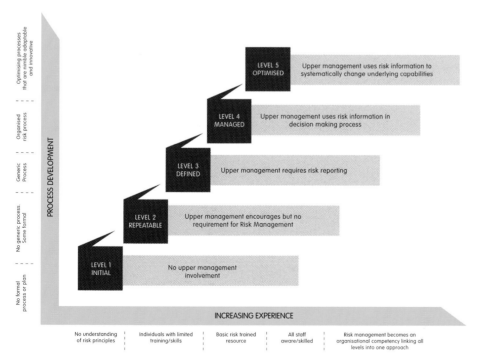

Figure 3.1 Clients should aim to become mature risk managers

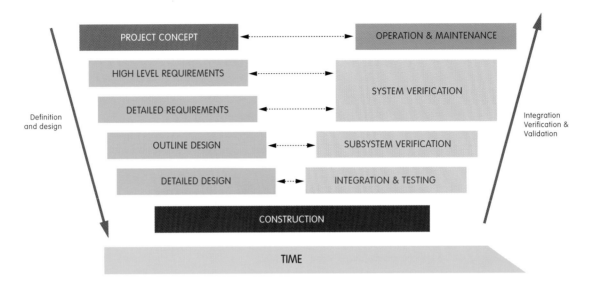

Figure 3.2. The systems-engineering 'V-lifecycle' of a project, in which each stage is verified and validated

Good data management can provide consistency, help the visibility and control interfaces, enable a detailed audit trail of the decision-making and accountability processes and set up a basis for as-built records and maintenance schedules. It can also provide ongoing feedback of performance in use. Design can be assembled as a 3D model or even 4D when correlated to construction planning and linked into Geographic Information System (GIS) databases. These can then be further linked to records of approvals and performance. If a visionary GIS system can be established at the outset it can be much more than an elaborate filing cabinet that facilitates data sharing. It is of most benefit on sites that are large or complex or will have several phases of development, when information sharing is difficult to achieve.

Good practice is to ensure that full records are kept of the project construction and that non-conformances with the project specification are methodically recorded, resolved and closed out. Records should include legacy photographs and any automated reporting systems or GIS.

Establishing the project database is therefore an activity which should be planned as early as possible as part of the project inception. Modern contracts such as those in the NEC3 suite (NEC, 2009) now also have aligned information management systems to help achieve tracking of instructions and acceptance.

If implemented at the outset and utilised throughout, a good database system together with a systems-engineering approach will assist to deliver project objectives more successfully.

'The processes established need to be flexible enough to cope with the demands of the project, and also be fully understood by both client and supply chain. There is no point in putting processes in place unless people understand them, and if they are not understood this will undermine the whole project.'
Construction industry specialist

Managing the programme and change

For many clients their biggest risk is adherence to programme. The project programme is an important tool for clients – time is money – and is under constant scrutiny. Clients should therefore ensure the programme is properly developed at the outset and in doing so make some risk-based assessment for programme contingency or float.

Change is almost inevitable in any project and can be imposed from either internal or external sources. Clients should be able to deal with this and also have change-control procedures in place as part of their systems engineering architecture, which can be instigated to assess and implement change as soon as it is identified. These will ensure that all implications of the change are addressed – cost, programme and interfaces (ref Associations of Project Management, 2006; Construction Clients' Group, 2008b).

Management of the programme can be controlled by reporting progress using specific, measurable, achievable, relevant and time-bound ('smart') objectives or targets.

'Things got off to a bad start when we did not have an adequate budget. We should have stopped things right there until we had got that sorted out. Instead we rushed into it. On most of our schemes now there would be a risk register that would have ensured before we started that it had an adequate budget. But on this scheme there was very little done to ensure that.' Client

Controlling costs

Many factors have an influence on cost. Clients should set up projects with factors that will make costs more controllable and give more certainty on outcome. The factors include:

> strong leadership

> clear objectives

> whole-life costing

> realistic budget with adequate risk and contingency pots

> achievable programme

> integrated team

> incentivisation

> systems-engineering approach

> change control

> risk management

> interface management

> non-adversarial form of contract.

Budgets have to be allocated fairly and monitored regularly together with risk and contingency pots.

Many clients use a quantified risk assessment in setting up the project budget, in which levels of confidence relating to the identified risks to cost and programme are evaluated and appropriate contingency allowances can be included. This should also identify the measures which can be taken to mitigate the risks.

Contingency allowances can be required to cover the following:

> resolution of incomplete information – in developing the details there are likely to be unforeseen elements

> overcoming circumstance that were not expected

> correcting errors

> needing to apply acceleration measures to the programme

Continued

Top ten items for ensuring project success

The following table provides a list of items which are considered to be the most important and require the client's attention during the course of the project.

No.	Item	Checks
1	Committed senior level support	Review project organisation Are the responsibilities of the investment decision makers and project sponsors clear? Has the Project Board signed off the project organisation and stakeholder analysis?
2	Proper initiation and project definition	Has the project scope been clearly defined and agreed? Have measurable success criteria been agreed? Has a risk plan been undertaken? Has a project initiation document been approved?
3	Flexible application of planning tools	Is the control and reporting system complex and cumbersome? Are the team members aware of their reporting responsibilities?
4	Realistic estimating and planning of resources	Has allowance been made for contingencies? Can task times be benchmarked? Is resource levelling between projects an issue? Is the task plan linked to the risk plan?
5	Project plan completed	Has the planning been structured to roll out through milestones? Has the integration of linked project tasks been undertaken? Production of the plan should not be rushed Consult and agree tasks and durations before committing to plan
6	Clear levels of authority	Project organisation document to state clearly responsibilities Level of decision-making and financial authority to be agreed and documented Have an internal audit undertaken of the project initiation
7	Clear roles and responsibilities	Job descriptions of Project Director and Core Project Team should be circulated to all team members and communicated to key stakeholders Consider team building days to clarify any concerns and identify team profiles
8	Good communications	A communication plan should be agreed by the Project Board and a team member given direct responsibility for its implementation
9	Good stakeholder management	Undertake a stakeholder analysis and commitment matrix Transfer this information into the communication plan Give someone specific responsibility to monitor and review the stakeholder profile
10	Control change	Establish this process at the very beginning Establish clear lines of authority to avoid unnecessary delay Communicate the process to the project team, design team and contractors Regularly monitor and review

> covering time-dependent costs associated with programme delay

> allowance for the introduction of recognised nominal extra requirements or 'scope growth'

> currency exchange rate movements

> indexing for inflation.

Not all of these may be relevant to a particular project, but these items are often the causes of additional costs.

It is also important for clients to establish as early as possible a cashflow forecast which should be monitored throughout the life of the project.

Summary

> Clients should have a clear vision of objectives and outcomes when developing the business case for their projects. The business case should include a realistic budget based on whole-life costs, a deliverable programme and a quantified risk register.

> Clients should consider adopting a structured systems engineering strategy for project delivery, including a project database.

> Clients should develop a detailed programme from the outset and set up change-control procedures as part of their overall cost-control process.

References

1. Actuarial Profession and Institution of Civil Engineers. *Strategic Risk: A Guide for Directors,* Thomas Telford, London, 2006.

2. Association for Project Management, *APM Body of Knowledge,* 5th ed., APM, London, 2006, www.apm.org.uk/BOK.asp

3. Construction Clients' Group. *Client's Commitments Best Practice Guide,* Chapter 3 Client leadership, Constructing Excellence, London, November 2008a. www.constructingexcellence.org.uk/sectorforums/constructionclientsgroup/clientcommitments/3.%20CL.pdf

4. Construction Clients' Group. *Client's Commitments Best Practice Guide,* Chapter 1: Procurement and integration, Constructing Excellence, London, November 2008b. www.constructingexcellence.org.uk/sectorforums/constructionclientsgroup/clientcommitments/1.%20Proc%20&%20Int.pdf

5. International Council on Systems Engineering. *Systems Engineering Handbook,* v3.1. www.incose.org

6. International Organization of Standardization. ISO IEC 15288:2002 Systems Engineering: System lifecycle processes.

7. NEC3. Various publications. www.neccontract.com

8. Office of Government Commerce. Whole-life Costing and Cost Management, CP0067, OGC, London, 2007a. www.ogc.gov.uk/documents/CP0067AEGuide7.pdf

9. Office of Government Commerce. *Risk and Value Management,* CP0064, OGC, London, 2007b. www.ogc.gov.uk/documents/CP0064AEGuide4.pdf

10. Saxon R. *Be Valuable: A Guide to Creating Value in the Built Environment,* Constructing Excellence, London, November 2005. www.saxoncbe.com/bevaluable.pdf

11. Woodcock H. UK Z-guides, Z1 – *What is Systems Engineering,* International Council on Systems Engineering, London, 2009. www.incoseonline.org.uk

Further reading

> Afila D. and Smith N. J. *Risk management and value management in project appraisal, Management, Procurement and Law,* 2007, 160, Issue 2.

> Kelly M. and Edmunds M. Channel Tunnel Rail Link section 2: project controls, *Civil Engineering,* 2007, 160, Issue 6.

> Constructing Excellence. *Lean Construction,* London 2006.

> Lewin C. Enterprise risk management and civil engineering, *Civil Engineering,* 2006, 159, Issue 6.

> Office of Government Commerce, *Managing Successful Programmes,* HMSO, 2007.

> Netlipse, network for the dissemination of knowledge on the management and organisation of large infrastructure projects in Europe. www.netlipse.eu/

> Winter M. and Checkland P. Soft systems: a fresh perspective for project management, *Civil Engineering,* 2003, 156, Issue 4.

> Wolstenholme A., Fugeman I. and Hammond F. *Heathrow Terminal 5: delivery strategy, Civil Engineering,* 2008, 161, Issue 5.

4.Establishing the client team

Contents

> *'I think one of the key aspects to the success of my project was that we always had the right resources. You have to have the right team and resource – this is not something that you should try to do on a shoe string.'*
> David Yeoell, Westminster City Council, Client

Large or small client team?

Clients have a decision to take at the outset of a project – whether to be closely involved in the decision making as the project progresses; or whether to set out clearly what they want, and appoint an external project management team in which they have complete confidence.

Valid reasons for having a small client team include:

> Construction is an important investment in the client's business but is peripheral to the activities and normal skillbase.

> Clients have done similar projects before and have established well-defined requirements and procedures.

> Clients have identified an external team with proven capabilities and an excellent reputation.

Other clients prefer to establish a large client team, which includes the project manager and permeates down into most levels of project management and delivery. Reasons could include:

> clients' core business is to conceive construction projects and manage them from inception to completion

> the project is complex and risky with clients having unique expertise in how to understand and manage it, so the client needs to be hands-on

> there are many external factors and stakeholders that clients have to handle directly to enable others to get on with the actual task of progressing the project.

There is no right answer: clients need to determine the approach that is right for them and their project (ref Office of Government Commerce, 2007a, 2007b; Construction Clients' Group, 2008a, 2008b; Construction Clients' Group and Business Vantage, 2009)

Figure 4.1. Clients need to decide on the extent of their client team from the outset – a bigger team requires more resources but gives greater control

Providing motivation

Whether part of a large or small team, high-performing client project people are the ones that deliver what the client wants.

The key to success is motivation. In terms of project work this can be defined as:

> *a cause* – something worthy to apply time and knowledge to

> *a leader* – someone to follow, to look up to, who drives things forward, provides clarity, makes decisions, removes obstacles

> *a valuable and valued role* – something that is clearly linked to the overall project objective, that is recognised for its worth, and that the team member is personally acknowledged and valued

> *empowerment to do the job* – to get on with the job, make decisions, support the client.

Motivation is one of the most powerful tools at the disposal of the team to deliver success. The client as a leader creates conditions for success in the client team as well as the overall delivery team.

'You can have systems and governance processes, but great projects are made by great people'.
Major Projects Association / ICE discussion on client best practice

Competencies and behaviours of project people

Less than 50% of people consulted in the preparation of this guide thought sufficient emphasis was given at the outset of a project to ensure the right competencies were built into their client teams.

The success of a construction project rests with the team charged with its delivery. Clients need to appreciate and understand the mutual respect needed to cement project-team relationships, and the importance of engaging the most appropriate project people. Of equal importance is the need for clients to understand when, in a project's lifecycle, they can add most value, as discussed in Chapter 2.

> *'Generally up to 80% of project success is attributed to people, what they do and particularly their behaviours in doing it. The challenge is that most of our effort goes into the other 20%, with the people matters considered to be so called 'soft issues' which can be dealt with tomorrow – but tomorrow never comes.'*
> John Lofty, JJL Consultancy Ltd, Client advisor

Smart project people drive best practice and feed back into the profession and industry. They are result-focused, strategic thinkers, rigorous analysers and planners, and pragmatists. These competencies need to be balanced with the attributes of the client team and the nature of a project over its lifecycle.

For example, strategic thinking at the planning and development phases of a project is crucial but, towards the end of the implementation phase, pragmatism and result-focused attitudes will be required. Equally, pragmatists can often scupper the solving of complex amorphous problems during the delivery of a project by reaching conclusions prematurely and not accepting the advice of the supply team.

Different client team skills are required at different points in a project's lifecycle; for example those good at the feasibility study/ design brief phase in the planning stage will not be as effective during the design phases of development and implementation stages when more detailed analysis and detailed rigorous justification are required.

Behaviours are more difficult to quantify and mould, and client team behaviour needs to be adaptable to fit each role in the lifecycle, so that, 'the client is someone you want to work for, not someone you have to work with' (Malcolm Noyse, Executive Director, Major Projects Association). For example, the planning element of a project's lifecycle requires intensive direction and drive from clients, whereas during the implementation period (assuming going to plan), the client team can be more relaxed.

Relationships are also key, and integrated working, particularly with the supply team, is of paramount importance (see Chapters 5 and 6).

> *'The leadership of the Hong Kong Mass Transit project was tough and single-minded, but it recognised that the project would only be successful if we created a team spirit across the organisation and with all other participants. This prevailed even in the midst of inevitable disagreements with contractors, banks and others. It was the team spirit that said "we either win together or we lose together".'* Professor Tony Ridley, first Managing Director of the KH Mass Transit Railway Corp.

Attraction and retention

From the detailed interviews carried out for this guide, 63% of respondents believed the right people were attracted to their projects, and 78% thought it was a very significant contribution to a project's success.

Clients need to attract the best project talent available and retain this for the duration of the required roles in a project's lifecycle. There are specific issues that clients take into account when attracting and retaining smart project people.

There is a tendency for types of projects to attract specialists, so clients need to have an awareness of the number of similar projects that will be underway in the proposed timeframe. Also, project people use their networks well to move from one job to another, so clients need to consider seeking the views of others as to where and how to locate the best personnel prior to launching a formal recruitment campaign.

High-prestige projects tend to attract the highest calibre of talent at the top echelons, but equally good, less-expensive talent can be found in the lower ranks. Networking through project management organisations and professional institutions, as well as government agency working groups, can augment specific knowledge.

Clients could consider endorsing non-standard working hours, health and wellbeing packages, good training and development, and extended holidays as part of the overall remuneration packages, or flex to suit individual requirements to get the best mix of project people (ref Constructing Excellence, 2004, 2006; Construction Clients' Group 2008c).

Figure 4.2. Clients need to attract the best people available and then motivate and retain them for the duration of the required roles in a project lifecycle

Project people are often so focused on the job in hand that they neglect their personal development. This has the plus side that they become extremely good at what they do, but the down side is that some may become disillusioned and less effective than they might be. Clients are advised to encourage the team to grow during a project by:

> promoting career development for project staff

> openly encouraging staff to plan their next assignments

> encouraging internal promotions in long-term projects

> promoting internal training sessions for improvement of technical and soft skills.

'I think projects are the best way of developing people – and there is a whole industry of people to develop. I am talking about throwing people in at the deep end to deal with the varying challenges of a project or a programme, and allowing and expecting them to make mistakes as long as they respond smartly, recover and make sure they are not making the same mistakes again. It is a marvellous opportunity and that is why I have some excellent people, because they have so much practice in the really good, high profile challenges. It is very worrying for them if they are the worrying kind, but once they have done a few, they begin to get a lot of confidence. It is a marvellous laboratory for developing people.'
Mike Nichols, the Nichols Group

Summary

> Clients need to decide how much of the project they wish to manage in-house and how much they wish to delegate to the project delivery team.

> They then need to put time and thought into creating a high-calibre client team consisting of people who are result-focused, strategic thinkers, rigorous analysers and planners, and pragmatists.

> If clients understand how the skills, behaviours, needs and aspirations of project people are unique, they will be able to attract and retain the best.

References

1. Constructing Excellence. *Respect for People: Reaching the Standard,* 3rd ed., Constructing Excellence, London, October 2004. www.constructingexcellence.org.uk/force_download. jsp?url=/pdf/rfp/rfp_Reaching_the_Standard.pdf

2. Constructing Excellence.. *Respect for People Toolkit,* Constructing Excellence, London, January 2006. www.constructingexcellence.org.uk/zones/peoplezone/ respect/respecttoolkits.jsp

3. Construction Clients' Group. *Client's Commitments Best Practice Guide,* Chapter 1 Procurement and integration, Constructing Excellence, London, November 2008a. www.constructingexcellence.org.uk/sectorforums/ constructionclientsgroup/clientcommitments/1.%20Proc%20 &%20Int.pdf

4. Construction Clients' Group. *Client's Commitments Best Practice Guide,* Chapter 3 Client leadership, Constructing Excellence, London, November 2008b. www.constructingexcellence. org.uk/sectorforums/constructionclientsgroup/ clientcommitments/3.%20CL.pdf

5. Construction Clients' Group and Business Vantage. *Equal Partners – Customer and Supplier Alignment in Private Sector Construction,* Business Vantage, Windsor, January 2009. www.constructingexcellence.org.uk/sectorforums/ constructionclientsgroup/reports/EP5.pdf

6. Office of Government Commerce. Project Organisation – Roles and Responsibilities, CP0062, OGC, London, 2007a. www.ogc.gov.uk/documents/CP0062AEGuide2.pdf

7. Office of Government Commerce. The Integrated Project Team – Teamworking and Partnering, CP0065, OGC, London, 2007b. www.ogc.gov.uk/documents/CP0065AEGuide5.pdf

8. Construction Clients' Group. *Client's Commitments Best Practice Guide,* Chapter 2 Commitment to people, Constructing Excellence, London, November 2008c. www.constructingexcellence.org.uk/sectorforums/ constructionclientsgroup/clientcommitments/2.%20C2P.pdf

Further reading

> HIPKISS A. Civil engineering career management – the unwritten rules, *Civil Engineering,* 2006, **159**, Issue 3.

> PLATTS J. and TOMASEVIC V. Developing productive relationships in civil engineering, *Civil Engineering,* **159**, Issue 3.

> SOETANTO R., PRICE A. and DAINTY A. *Improving management of people in construction, Management, Procurement and Law,* 2007, **160**, Issue 1.

5.Procuring the supply team

Contents

> *'Given the responsibility that most clients pass to their supply chain [via the project manager] to deliver their projects, making sure that the right organisations are attracted in the first place seems to be one of the most important elements of the client role.'*
> Rosemary Beales, Civil Engineering Contractors Association

Defining a procurement strategy

Clients will know what they want as an outcome from their project but they have to decide at an early stage how best to achieve this through their procurement strategy. Having the procurement strategy properly aligned with the project objectives as described in the business case is essential. The essence of a good procurement strategy is to set out and define the right process to achieve these objectives. The selected approach can influence the confidence in the business case and the chances of the project being more successful.

The procurement strategy is key to defining how the project is to be delivered. It should make clear how the engagement of advisors, design consultants, suppliers and contractors is to be undertaken. It should also make clear under what contractual arrangements these appointments are to be made.

The procurement strategy should typically include the following:

> basis for seeking tenders, eg. full design and then construct, design and build, PFI/PPP, etc

> work packaging – the number of contracts and work breakdown between contracts

> publicity to attract the right level of interest from the market

> process for bidder prequalification and short-listing

> bid and evaluation processes, including timeframe

> criteria used for scoring and comparing bids

> attitude to risk allocation and contingencies

> process for accepting winning bids

> terms of engagement/forms of contract

> roles and responsibilities (eg. health and safety).

One of the biggest challenges for clients in developing the strategy is to bring on board suppliers to help them deliver their project successfully (ref Office of Government Commerce, 2007a, 2007b; Construction Clients' Group, 2008). Depending on the extent and capability of the client team (see Chapter 4) and the method chosen for procuring the project, suppliers can include any or all of the following:

> funding advisors

> legal advisors

> insurers

> media and public relations specialists

> planning and environmental consultants

> health and safety advisors

> architectural and engineering designers

> project manager/project controls

> cost managers

> contractors

> specialist trades, suppliers and manufacturers

> facilities managers.

Many clients choose a 'two envelope' approach to procuring services. This involves the tenderers submitting a 'quality' submission as well as a commercial submission. The quality submission will cover, among other things, methodologies and team structure. Clients assess these submissions on best value or most economically advantageous tender which normally means a scoring system for assessing the submissions with a split of say 70% on the quality submission and 30% on the commercial. This displays a client's commitment to not just accepting lowest price.

Some clients are now using a technique called competitive dialogue where the client will usually request a shortlist of three tenderers, following prequalification, to enter into a dialogue individually with the client. During the dialogue period, dialogue in respect of each participant's developing outline proposals takes place between the client and each participant as to the acceptability or otherwise of their outline proposals. Matters to be discussed between the client and each participant during the dialogue period normally include (but may not be limited to):

(a) compliance with required standards

(b) impact of proposals on environmental issues

(c) traffic management

(d) clarification of tender documents

(e) consideration of basis for design

(f) parliamentary process

(g) aesthetics

(h) quality assurance

(i) cooperation requirements

(j) health and safety/sustainability

(k) developing outline proposals

(l) conformance with the employer's requirements

(m) inspection and testing requirements.

Subject to compliance with the competitive dialogue process, all participants should receive a letter of invitation to submit a final tender together with the final tender documents.

Whichever procurement method is chosen, it is normally the case that clients will offer unsuccessful tenderers the opportunity to request a debriefing from the client.

Avoiding the 'procurement trap'

Problems can result when the pre-qualification process requires suppliers to demonstrate complex in-house management practices and procedures, as these may form an obstacle to the very firms with the necessary expertise for the project. It can result in these specialists becoming involved as subcontractors to other larger organisations. This has the net effect of making the skills that can add real value to the project being at least one-step removed from the client, with an intermediary who has less expertise, imposing an additional cost purely to satisfy the prequalification criteria, unless the main contractor positively facilitates the specialist/client interface.

Clients should ensure that the level of competition for work is appropriate. So, a good test for the procurement strategy is to ask: 'Are those who are best able to do the work enabled by the proposed approach to actually win the contracts?'

Packaging up the work

In some cases it is beneficial to award complete, all-inclusive packages. In others, where the work has to be installed in a complex sequence of stages with external interdependencies, it may be more flexible to split the scope into discrete work packages.

The procurement strategy should seek to optimise this situation, as follows:

> minimise the number of interfaces between contract packages

> place and define required interfaces between contract packages so that they will be relatively easy to control and manage

> introduce specific, managed interfaces where this will permit an increased confidence in the successful delivery of the overall project, or an improved control of the overall final cost

> analyse interfaces rigorously to ensure there are no gaps

> allow early work packages to be tendered and awarded to suit the programme and more complex packages to continue to be developed, so as better to define their scope and/or mitigate potential risks

> enable different contract conditions to be used to suit the different elements of work

> enable the selection of 'construction only' for some contracts and 'design and build' for others

> allow suppliers to be selected to match the skills and capabilities required for different works and thus achieve improved confidence in their performance and more competitive pricing

> enable risks to be allocated differently between client and supplier for different work packages, placing risks with those organisations most able to manage them and thus control the final price and programme

> split or subdivide work so that more suppliers have the ability to price for it, spreading the risk of delivery and/or to enable smaller suppliers with lower cost structures to undertake elements of the work cost-effectively

> understand and define who is responsible for any slack in the programme between the project packages to avoid disputes should one overrun to the detriment of others

> arrange packages of work so they can be commissioned and handed over early, either to allow follow-on contracts to proceed cleanly, or to enable the commencement of operation.

Choosing the right procurement method

The procurement strategy needs to identify how and when suppliers are brought onto the project. There are numerous procurement methods that have developed over time for use by construction clients as shown in Table 5.1.

	Description
Traditional	Contractor appointed to deliver a defined set of works
Two-stage	Contractor chosen on basis of limited information before negotiating final deal
Early contractor involvement	Contractor appointed early, often in parallel with design team
Construction management	Appoint construction manager to oversee works delivered by trade contractors in direct relationship with client
Framework	Appoint supplier on basis of competencies, quality of services and rates, which are then applied to various projects over the life of the framework
Design and build	Client appoints contractor to deliver both design and construction of project
Design build finance operate	Public sector client appoints contractor to fund, design, construct and maintain building or structure for long-term concession

Table 5.1. Procurement methods

There are advantages and disadvantages in the different options and clients need to understand these to be able to make an informed decision. Factors to consider or amplify in considering the right option include:

> timing of obtaining a contractual commitment and binding price

> need or otherwise to overlap design with construction

> need for a single point of responsibility

> no ambiguity over safety and the degree to which this is delegated down the supply chain

> need for supplier input into complex construction sequencing

> spend profile between the design phase and the construction phase

> complexity of design approvals and sign-off before committing to construction

> how the project is funded

> relative importance of cost, programme and quality

> who is in control of quality and design excellence.

Choosing the right form of contract

The procurement strategy will set out which type of contract is recommended for each of the packages. The choice of contract will be determined by the nature of the works.

However, best practice generally means using a contract that encourages collaborative working. The UK Office of Government Commerce suggests the use of the ICE's suite of NEC3 (ref NEC, 2009) contracts for this purpose. Other forms of contract which can be used include JCT or GC Works.

Figure 5.1. The UK Office of Government Commerce suggests the use of the ICE's suite of collaborative NEC3 contracts for all contracts with suppliers

Achieving statutory approvals

Another major consideration in developing the procurement strategy and in defining the work packages will be the ability to achieve planning consent and other statutory approvals. Proceeding without approvals in place is a major risk and one that suppliers cannot reasonably be expected to manage. They may be expected to manage and close-out the details of 'reserved matters' and other conditions associated with the consents but not the overall risk of gaining approvals.

If work packages are contracted before there is adequate close-out of consents and approvals then any material changes that are required to satisfy the authorities provide the supplier with a reason for variation and delay. This can be avoided by packaging the project so that works for which adequate approvals have been obtained can be progressed and contracts awarded, while the consents for other later packages are still being negotiated.

Communicating clearly

Clients should communicate with potential suppliers (including key subcontractors) well before the procurement part of the implementation stage, with information flowing in both directions. By providing an early insight into their intentions and building a relationship with the market prior to procurement, they benefit from expert input in the development of a project and ensure suppliers are geared up to meet project demands (ref Office of Government Commerce, 2006).

If clients are able to provide a clear understanding of what their core business activity and strategy are, they should reasonably expect suppliers to ensure that they understand this, and take steps to match their bid to clients' requirements.

Market engagement can take many forms, including regular supplier conferences and newsletters, bidder days and the use of prior information notices in the *Official Journal of the European Union.*

Clients should provide feedback to their suppliers on their performance using key performance indicators (see Chapter 7). They should also encourage suppliers to give feedback about any issues that may have arisen. Having shared this feedback, clients and their suppliers should look for areas of improvement and, once established, set revised goals.

Case study – Scottish infrastructure investment plan

The Scottish government has committed to produce a document every three years giving details of every infrastructure project valued at more than £5 million to be delivered in the country over the following decade. By publishing this document, the government is able to offer infrastructure suppliers in Scotland a clear indication of where anticipated investment will be during this period, allowing much better business planning and identification of any potential 'pinch-points' for resources and skills (ref Scottish Government, 2008).

Understanding your suppliers

Just as it is important to provide information to suppliers, effective clients will also want to have an informed view of both those suppliers they chose to work with, and the wider construction industry.

During the planning and development stages, clients must ensure that the supply market will be able to deliver their project or programme of works. As well as the obvious requirements in terms of resources and supplier capacity, clients should also be sure that they understand whether their suppliers have the technical ability to meet the demands of a project, and that there is sufficient interest from suppliers to ensure reasonable competition for the works.

Where it is recognised that there are shortfalls in any particular skill or resource, clients must make a decision on how they intend to address this, either by amending their proposals to allow for this shortfall, looking to encourage suppliers to develop new capabilities or – in the worst case scenario – consider whether this shortfall means a project can no longer go ahead. Where specific resources are scarce, or have long lead times, it is vital clients are aware of this at an early stage allowing them to secure these resources without affecting the programme.

As a project moves into the implementation stage, clients, or their representatives, should still retain this understanding both of their individual suppliers and the wider market. By doing so, clients can identify and mitigate problems, such as a supplier getting into financial difficulty or escalating costs caused by an unexpected shortage of market capacity (ref Office of Government Commerce, 2008; Business Vantage, 2009).

Collaborative working and integrated teams

Most current procurement processes can be described as either 'traditional' or 'collaborative'. Traditional approaches involve detailed designs and specifications being prepared to allow procurement upon the basis of 'lowest price'. This method of procurement works well for simple 'prescribed' construction projects where 'offer' and 'acceptance' can be clearly identified.

When applied to complex construction projects (i.e. those with multiple trades), traditional procurement methods can provide difficulties in defining the complexities of the project works. This can lead to disputes between the parties over what was actually procured and how it was described. Clients often find final costs do not match the tender costs in these instances.

For complex construction in particular, clients should consider a 'collaborative procurement' approach (ref Major Projects Association, 2001; Strategic Forum for Construction, 2003; Office of Government Commerce, 2007c, 2007d; Strategic Forum for Construction, 2007). Collaborative procurement goes beyond the 'offer and acceptance' style of traditional method towards more negotiated methodology based upon performance terms. An example of the benefits of this approach can be demonstrated by looking at clients' approach to risk. As discussed in Chapter 3, construction projects often encompass considerable risk, both to the client as well as the supply chain and wider stakeholders.

Traditional procurement often seeks to place all the risk within the supply chain through prescriptive terms. This risk transfer is priced by suppliers and incorporated within their tender sums. A collaborative procurement approach allows the parties to negotiate both value- and cost-efficient solutions in relation to these risks.

Risk can be identified more easily within an integrated team working together on a construction project, and risk ownership can be discussed more openly with a greater emphasis on mitigation. Where risk remains it can be shared by the parties. Clients may wish to retain all risks to benefit from cheaper tender sums.

Having appointed suppliers, clients should then integrate them as part of a single project team and aim to develop relationships between individual team members. Through such integration, clients can exploit the skills of individual suppliers for the benefit of a project. Successful integrated teams thrive in an environment where all parties work together in a spirit of trust and openness. As yet such behaviour is not commonplace in the industry and, for this reason, clients and their suppliers may initially have to expend significant efforts towards changing the culture within their organisations to achieve harmonious integration.

Such collaborative working, often with all parties working out of the same offices, will result in people working together to deliver a project rather than merely looking after the interests of their own organisations. Clients should also instil a 'no-blame' culture within the integrated team, recognising that it is better to identify and deal with problems rather than unknowingly let them fester. They also provide a well-established and understood method for resolving any problems that do arise.

In many cases clients may only have a contractual relationship with a single main supplier, which will take responsibility for management of the lower-tier suppliers that will work on a project. This supplier should exhibit the same principles of client best practice outlined in this guide in its role as client to these sub-tier firms.

Case study – collaboration underpins programme effectiveness at Farringdon Station

Farringdon Station re-development is the point at which Thameslink, CrossRail and London Underground routes will intersect, making this the first station to have direct access to three of London's airports – Heathrow, Gatwick and Luton. The programme is highly complex in terms of maintaining operational continuity for the travelling public, integration of engineering solutions, the range of specialist teams involved and the criticality of achieving timelines.

> 'We have brought the client and supply teams together as a leadership group early in the programme to define the strategy in terms of goals, objectives and measures of success. This level of close collaboration is already paying dividends to the effectiveness of the programme.'
> Richard Walker, Network Rail Programme Manager

Rewarding for delivery

Clients should agree a structure for payment for all works carried out (ref Office of Government Commerce, 2007). As part of this process, they may look to incentivise suppliers to achieve the best possible results. Equally, they may include a way of ensuring that any losses occurring are shared across the project team. Any such 'pain/gain share' arrangements must be clearly stated and agreed from the outset.

Following completion of works, clients should aim to make payment promptly to an agreed schedule and ensure that this payment is passed down to all members of the supply chain. Clients should avoid stretching payment terms or withholding payment through the use of retentions if the work has been carried out to the agreed specification.

Raising quality and finding better ways of working

Good design can dramatically improve the quality of the construction project. Good construction procurement should therefore consider quality across the full project lifecycle.

Good design should be functional as well as aesthetically pleasing. The balance between visual appearance and

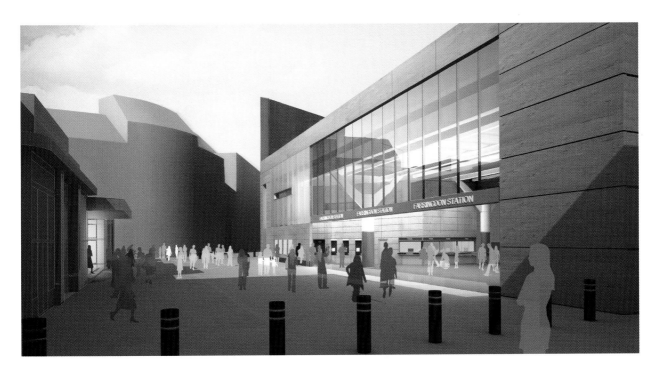

Figure 5.2. Farringdon station redevelopment in London, where client and supply teams were together early to define project goals, objectives and measures of success

efficiency is often difficult for clients to fully define at the outset, so utilisation of a design professional is advised (ref Office of Government Commerce, 2007e; Construction Clients' Group, 2008; also see www.cabe.org.uk; www.architecture.com; www. betterpublicbuilding.org.uk; www.dqui.org.uk; www.cic.org.uk).

The overall construction project can be measured for quality through the use of a national benchmarking standard. The Constructing Excellence key performance indicators measure the industry each year and offer the client a choice of measurements across economic, social and environmental standards (see www. kpizone.com; www.ccinw.com/sites/kpi_index.html?site_id=5).

Clients with a series of projects can harness benefits that can be achieved by continuous improvement. They can agree challenging targets with suppliers for improvements over a series of projects in areas such as the cost and time taken to deliver standard elements. These improvements should be achieved by driving out inefficiency, rather than by merely demanding suppliers reduce their costs by cutting margins.

As part of the continuous improvement process, suppliers should be encouraged to train and develop their employees to improve their capabilities and performance, and clients may have a role to play in facilitating this training where there is a common requirement among a number of suppliers.

Clients should also expect their suppliers to demonstrate a commitment to innovation to secure improvements, without risking the success of their projects through the use of novel and untested methods, processes or technologies (ref Network Rail, 2007; Office of Government Commerce, 2007f).

In return for demonstrating continuous improvement, clients should reward well-performing integrated project teams with direct financial incentives or the benefit of continuity of workload. By allowing the negotiation of repeat business on this basis, clients reduce both the financial cost and the time taken to tender work.

Summary

> Clients should develop a clearly defined procurement strategy that allows those suppliers best suited to working on a project to win contracts to deliver it.

> Clients should maintain open dialogue with suppliers, both as they develop their proposals for a project or programme of works and also during delivery. This communication should be two-way, with suppliers providing their expert knowledge to secure more efficient delivery of the project.

> Clients should ensure that they understand whether the capabilities and capacity that exist among suppliers will meet the demands of their project, and take steps to address the issue where this is not the case.

> Complex projects in particular are best tackled by client and supply teams collaborating as part of an integrated team.

> Clients and suppliers should agree a fair structure for payment, which must be adhered to following satisfactory completion of the works according to the agreed structure.

> Suppliers and clients should work together to establish standards of quality on projects and then seek to improve upon these standards through a commitment to training and innovation.

References

1. Business Vantage. *Equal Partners – Customer and Supplier Alignment in Private Sector Construction*, 2009. www.businessvantage.co.uk/equalpartners/Equal%20Partners%202009.pdf

2. Construction Clients' Group. *Client's Commitments Best Practice Guide*, Chapter 1 Procurement and integration, Constructing Excellence, London, November 2008a. www.constructingexcellence.org.uk/sectorforums/constructionclientsgroup/clientcommitments/1.%20Proc%20&%20Int.pdf

3. Construction Clients' Group. *Client's Commitments Best Practice Guide*, Chapter 5 Design quality, Constructing Excellence, London, November 2008b. www.constructingexcellence.org.uk/sectorforums/constructionclientsgroup/clientcommitments/5.%20DQ.pdf

4. Major Projects Association. *Effective Teams for Complex Projects*, 2001. www.majorprojects.org/pubdoc/670.pdf

5. NEC3 (various publications), 2009. www.neccontract.co.uk

6. Network Rail. *Intelligent Infrastructure Good Practice Guide*, 2007. www.networkrail.co.uk/documents/4350_IntelligentInfrastructureGoodPracticeGuide.pdf

7. Office of Government Commerce. The Integrated Project Team, Teamworking and Partnering, 2003. www.ogc.gov.uk/documents/CP0065AEGuide5.pdf

8. Office of Government Commerce. *Early Market Engagement – Principals and Examples of Good Practice*, 2006. www.ogc.gov.uk/documents/Early_market_engagement-Principles_examples_good_practice.pdf

9. Office of Government Commerce. Project Procurement Lifecycle – the Integrated Process, CP0063, OGC, London, 2007a. www.ogc.gov.uk/documents/CP0063AEGuide3.pdf

10. Office of Government Commerce. Procurement and Project Strategies, CP0066, OGC, London, 2007b. www.ogc.gov.uk/documents/CP0066AEGuide6.pdf

11. Office of Government Commerce. The Integrated Project Team – Teamworking and Partnering, CP0065, OGC, London, 2007c. www.ogc.gov.uk/documents/CP0065AEGuide5.pdf

12. Office of Government Commerce. Guide to Best 'Fair Payment' Practices, CP0159, OGC, London, 2007d. www.ogc.gov.uk/documents/CP0159FairPaymentPractices.pdf

13. Office of Government Commerce. Design Quality, CP0069, OGC, London, 2007e. www.ogc.gov.uk/documents/CP0069AEGuide9.pdf

14. Office of Government Commerce. Improving Performance, CP0068, OGC, London, 2007f. www.ogc.gov.uk/documents/CP0068AEGuide8.pdf

15. Office of Government Commerce. *Category Management Toolkit Supply Market Research*, 2008. www.ogc.gov.uk/documents/Supply_Market_Research(1).pdf

16. Scottish Government, The. *Infrastructure Investment Plan 2008*, 2008. www.scotland.gov.uk/Resource/Doc/217601/0058293.pdf

17. Strategic Forum for Construction. *Integration Toolkit*, 2003. www.strategicforum.org.uk/sfctoolkit2/home/home.html

18. Strategic Forum for Construction. *Profiting from Integration, Construction Industry Council*, London, November 2007. www.strategicforum.org.uk/pdf/ITGReport120308.pdf

Further reading

> Afila D. and Smith N. J. Risk management and value management in project appraisal, *Management, Procurement and Law*, 2007, **160**, Issue 2.

> Attridge M. and Tamber H. Channel Tunnel Rail Link section 2: procurement and contract strategy, *Civil Engineering*, 2007, **160**, Issue 6.

> Bayley M. Channel Tunnel Rail Link: financing and risk transfer, *Civil Engineering*, 2003, **156**, Issue 5.

> Blockley D. and Godfrey P. Measuring judgements to improve performance, *Civil Engineering*, 2005, **158**, Issue 3.

> Cathcart A. Channel Tunnel Rail Link: a contract partnership, *Civil Engineering*, 2003, **156**, Issue 5.

> Fryer S. How to achieve true quality in construction, *Management, Procurement and Law*, 2007, **160**, Issue 1.

> Griffith A. and Bhutto K. Contractors' experiences of integrated management systems, *Management, Procurement and Law*, 2008, **161**, Issue 3.

> Hamilton A. Project design: tasks that need to be managed, *Management, Procurement and Law*, 2008, **161**, Issue 3.

> Hawkins J. and Wells J. How infrastructure procurement can enhance social development, *Management, Procurement and Law*, 2007, **160**, Issue 1.

> Keeling D. Channel Tunnel Rail Link: quality management, *Civil Engineering*, 2003, **156**, Issue 5.

> Leiper Q. and Pepper C. From securing to procuring our future, *Civil Engineering*, 2007, **160**, Issue 1.

> Lewin C. Enterprise risk management and civil engineering, *Civil Engineering*, 2006, **159**, Issue 6.

> Morris P. W. G. Science, objective knowledge and the theory of project management, *Civil Engineering*, 2002, **150**, Issue 2.

> Mustow S. E. Procurement of ethical construction products, *Engineering Sustainability*, 2006, **159**, Issue 1.

> Paton J. Making the case for collaboration in civil engineering, *Civil Engineering*, 2002, **150**, Issue 6.

> Phillips M. A value and risk management approach to project development, *Civil Engineering*, 2002, **150**, Issue 2.

> Shelbourn M. A. Framework for effective collaborative working in construction et al., *Management, Procurement and Law*, 2007, **160**, Issue 4.

> Stonehouse J. Delivering value in public sector construction, *Civil Engineering*, 2007, **160**, Issue 1.

> Stovin V., Eccles S. and O'Reilly M. Choosing the right contract: a probabilistic model, *Civil Engineering*, 2004, **157**, Issue 2.

> Wamuziri S. and Madan S. Improvement and innovation through collaborative partnerships, *Management, Procurement and Law*, 2009, **162**, Issue 1.

6. Caring for people and the environment

Contents

'Along with its suppliers, clients should also ensure clear communication with other organisations and individuals that will have an influence over the project or be impacted by it. Key stakeholders are likely to include communities in the area surrounding the project site, funders, occupiers, users and their customers.'
Project manager

Benefits to society

Leading client organisations are increasingly aware of the impact they have on people and the environment and of the opportunities and obligations they have to be a 'force for good' in society. Indeed, for many clients, being a 'force for good' becomes part of the strategic intent for their project.

Social impact includes not only the construction period, but also the performance delivered by the asset. Clients should identify their social opportunities and obligations at the earliest planning stage – including safety, health, environment, sustainability, quality of life, equality, diversity, access and inclusion.

Safety, health and environment

The safety, health and environmental aspects of construction projects are all governed by primary legislation, case law and tort. In the UK this is as follows:

> safety: Health and Safety at Work Act (1974) with its duty of care

> health: Health and Safety at Work Act and extension of occupational health into the construction industry

> environment: Control of Pollution Act (1974).

However, clients should set boundaries of acceptability that are tighter than the legislation.

Clients also have specific legal responsibilities under the Construction Design and Management (CDM) Regulations, which make them accountable for the impact a project has on health and safety. Principally, they must appoint a competent CDM coordinator; ensure adequacy of information, management arrangements, time and resource to allow safe delivery (ref Construction Industry Training Board, 2007).

Safety and health

Clients should develop, articulate and believe in a strong safety culture, instilled into people's behaviours, and then give a clear indication of expectations in line with this culture – and of their willingness to pay to achieve it (ref Saxon, 2005; Office of Government Commerce, 2007a; Construction Clients' Group, 2008a). They should have a genuine level of belief, without which the converse is also invariably true, resulting in a cost-cutting race to the bottom. Without strong leadership, good practice can get crowded out by supply chain competition, with suppliers attempting to cut corners on what are ultimately moral issues.

Clients should address design for safety early for it to have the best effect. They should consider using early contractor involvement (see Chapter 5) to enable suppliers to have a valuable input into safety of construction methods and long-term operation and maintenance.

In planning for safety, clients should be the guiding mind, able to foresee every construction process and its safe execution. They should consider using safety-related key performance indicators

(KPIs), such as training delivered ('lead KPI') and accident frequency rates ('lag KPI'), as a part of the contractual payment process. They should also encourage a behavioural approach while retaining rules to enable policing, and facilitate peer pressure.

Clients should use occupational health screening within their accident-reduction strategy. They should consider investing in medical staff to improve productivity and commitment, and using screening to give a message to the whole workforce that they – the workforce – are important.

Case study – safety at Heathrow T5

The £4.3 billion Heathrow Terminal 5 project achieved a safety performance four times better than industry norms, whilst employing over 60 000 construction workers. A cultural change was created by using safety leadership – as distinct from safety management – coupled with real engagement of, and respect for, all concerned. Communications initiatives included a monthly health and safety newspaper and an 'injury and incident free' programme (ref Evans, 2008).

Environment

Clients should seek to minimise adverse impact on the environment during both construction and operation phases (ref Saxon, 2005; Office of Government, 2007b; Construction Clients' Group, 2008b; HM Government and Strategic Forum for Construction, 2008). Early engagement of the supply team will often be helpful in this.

Independent validation can be provided by the Civil Engineering Environmental Quality Assessment and Award Scheme (ref CEEQUAL, 2009), which has become the accepted UK industry scheme for assessing environmental and sustainability performance in civil engineering and public realm projects, and can also be used to improve these aspects of a project. The CEEQUAL *Assessment Manual for Projects* contains the 200 questions that comprise the CEEQUAL scheme and against which projects are assessed. The *Manual* also contains background information and references, guidance on scoring and scoping out,

and examples of what is considered appropriate evidence. The question set is split into the following 12 topic areas:

> project management

> land use

> landscape

> ecology and biodiversity

> the historic environment

> water resources and the water environment

> energy and carbon

> material use

> waste management

> transport

> effects on neighbours

> relations with the local community and other stakeholders.

Similarly, for buildings, the most widely used scheme is the BRE Environmental Assessment Method (BREEAM) (ref BRE Global Ltd, 2009).

BREEAM sets a standard for best practice in sustainable design and is a measure used to describe a building's environmental performance. It provides clients, developers, designers and others with:

> market recognition for low environmental impact buildings

> assurance that best environmental practice is incorporated into a building

> inspiration to find innovative solutions that minimise the environmental impact

> a benchmark that is higher than regulation

> a tool to help reduce running costs, improve working and living environments

> a standard that demonstrates progress towards corporate and organisational environmental objectives.

Incident and injury free

They're proud of you too

You have people who count on you to get home safely each night - your kids, your wife, your parents.
Take care, so that you can go home safely to your family.

Make T5 Safe.

Figure 6.1. Clients should develop and articulate a strong safety culture – this poster campaign was one of many such initiatives at the ultra-safe Heathrow Terminal 5 site

Environmental issues that clients should consider include the following:

> *Waste.* Clients need to understand the relevant waste legislation and the issues behind it. For example, site waste management plans place a clear responsibility on clients to initiate excellence by eliminating waste in design (ref Waste and Resources Action Programme, 2009).

> *Recycling.* Clients should encourage maximum use of recycled materials by avoiding over-prescriptive specification and motivating the supply chain to increase its use of recycling.

> *Environmental issues.* Most projects require extensive environmental input. This will normally be in the form of environmental impact assessments and environmental surveys, many of which are required as part of the planning legislation. Clients should investigate these issues early, as some surveys may need to be made years in advance of a project starting on site.

See also Chapter 8 on legacy and sustainability issues.

Quality of life

Quality of life issues embrace both the project team and the local community (ref Constructing Excellence, 2004, 2007). Genuine care for the local community benefits the community and the project. Clients should encourage a user-friendly attitude from the project team towards the community, placing emphasis on environmental measures that affect quality of life, such as noise, dust and traffic. This also engenders good relations with environmental health officers.

Clients should consider using local meetings, press releases, literature mailshots, local radio and so on to generate confidence within the community. This leads to fewer complaints and minimises any negative press. Clients should also embrace new technology – such as web logs, text messaging and RSS feeds – to communicate across construction project teams and with the local community. Many communities use local networking sites on the internet – engaging with these websites to keep people informed of construction activity is valued, and at minimal cost (ref Abbott, 2007).

Early involvement of the supply team allows clients to speak with confidence about key aspects of detail in the delivery process, assuaging anxiety and turning nervous criticism to support (see Chapter 5) (ref Considerate Constructors Scheme, 2008).

Equality and diversity

Many equality and diversity issues are enshrined in legislation, with prohibitions against discrimination (ref Constructing Excellence, 2004, 2006). Clients need to be passionate about these issues and able to mentor and encourage their supply chain regarding the benefits of diversity. They should set the vision, such as local employment or training to re-skill local people, and then engage with and encourage suppliers. This vision will also encourage suppliers to recognise that diversity within a workforce is a source of strength, but based on meritocracy within a principled commitment to diversity, measured by attitude and behaviours, rather than mere box ticking with quotas as demonstration of compliance.

Clients should encourage their delivery teams to avoid a systemic lack of diversity in management processes by ensuring there is no inherent bias in selection for training and development, or reward and recognition. If job advertisements are overtly diverse, this approach can easily be maintained through the selection process – which is preferable to applying diversity late in the process.

Access and inclusion of local supply chain

Clients should promote access and inclusion. They should consider fostering links with local schools, including site visits, which generate interest, involvement and ultimately employment in the industry.

In a challenging economic environment, projects can be leveraged to benefit the local community – particularly in areas of high unemployment – by encouraging the project team to promote local employment, upskilling the local workforce, developing the local economic base, and giving the community a more sustainable basis for its future.

Case study – access to work for the long-term economically inactive in the Rhondda Valley

Client leadership encouraged tendering contractors to consider training and employing people who had not worked before. Early contractor involvement enabled the contractor to think creatively about ways to engage with the unemployed. Successful training and employment of 46 long-term unemployed people gave inspiration to the local community, and generated new and enthusiastic employees, 14 of whom relocated at the end of the contract to remain in the contractor's employment.

Figure 6.2. Clients should consider fostering links with local schools to help generate community support for their projects and, ultimately, a source of future suppliers

Summary

> Clients should recognise their impact on society, and the opportunities and obligations they have, particularly to the people employed or affected by their project.

> Clients should take a proactive role in setting and communicating a visionary agenda for issues such as safety and health, environmental aspects, sustainability, quality of life, equality, diversity, access and inclusion.

References

1. Abbott M. Managing the inner world of infrastructure, *Civil Engineering*, 2007, **160** Issue 1.

2. BRE Global Ltd. *BRE Environmental Assessment Method*, 2009. www.breeam.org

3. Civil Engineering Environmental Quality Assessment and Award Scheme, 2009. www.ceequal.org.uk

4. Considerate Constructors Scheme, 2008. www.considerateconstructorsscheme.org.uk/

5. Constructing Excellence. *Respect for People: Reaching the Standard,* 3rd ed., Constructing Excellence, London, October 2004. www.constructingexcellence.org.uk/force_download.jsp?url=/pdf/rfp/rfp_Reaching_the_Standard.pdf

6. Constructing Excellence. *Respect for People Toolkit,* Constructing Excellence, London, January 2006. www.constructingexcellence.org.uk/zones/peoplezone/respect/respecttoolkits.jsp

7. Construction Industry Training Board. The Construction (Design and Management) Regulations 2007: Industry Guidance for Small, One-off and Infrequent Clients, CDM07/1, Construction Skills, King's Lynn, June 2007. www.constructingexcellence.org.uk/sectorforums/constructionclientsgroup/downloads/final_cdm_guidance_21June07.pdf

8. Construction Clients' Group. *Client's Commitments Best Practice Guide,* Chapter 6 Health and safety, Constructing Excellence, London, November 2008a. www.constructingexcellence.org.uk/sectorforums/constructionclientsgroup/clientcommitments/6.%20H&S.pdf

9. Construction Clients' Group. *Health and Safety Key Performance Indicators,* Construction Excellence, London, July 2008b. www.constructingexcellence.org.uk/sectorforums/constructionclientsgroup/downloads/CCG%20KPI%27s%20for%20Industry.pdf

10. Construction Clients' Group. *Client's Commitments Best Practice Guide,* Chapter 4 Sustainability, Constructing Excellence, London, November 2008c. www.constructingexcellence.org.uk/sectorforums/constructionclientsgroup/clientcommitments/4.%20Sust.pdf

11. Evans M. Heathrow Terminal 5: health and safety leadership, *Civil Engineering*, 2008, **161**, Issue 5.<AQ52>

12. HM Government and Strategic Forum for Construction. *Strategy for Sustainable Construction,* Department for Business, Enterprise and Regulatory Reform, London, June 2008. www.berr.gov.uk/files/file46535.pdf

13. Office of Government Commerce. *Health and Safety,* CP0070, OGC, London, 2007a. www.ogc.gov.uk/documents/CP0070AEGuide10.pdf

14. Office of Government Commerce. Sustainability, CP0016, OGC, London, 2007b. www.ogc.gov.uk/documents/CP0016AEGuide11.pdf

15. Saxon R. *Be Valuable: A Guide to Creating Value in the Built Environment,* Constructing Excellence, London, November 2005. www.saxoncbe.com/bevaluable.pdf

16. Waste and Resources Action Programme (Wrap), 2009. www.wrap.org.uk

Further reading

> Donaghy R. *One death is too many, Report to the Secretary of State for Work and Pension,* July 2009. www.official-documents.gov.uk/document/cm76/7657/7657.pdf

> French S. Channel Tunnel Rail Link: the case for safety, *Civil Engineering*, 2003, **156**, Issue 5.

> Gambrill B. Channel Tunnel Rail Link: community relations during implementation, *Civil Engineering*, 2003, **156**, Issue 5.

> Hawkins J. and Wells J. How infrastructure procurement can enhance social development, *Management, Procurement and Law*, 2007, **160**, Issue 1.

> Kalowski J. Community consultation: lessons from Sydney. *Management, Procurement and Law*, 2008, **161**, Issue 2.

> Kennerley J. A. Channel Tunnel Rail Link: the complaints commissioner, *Civil Engineering*, 2003, **156**, Issue 5.

> Mustow S. E. Procurement of ethical construction products, *Engineering Sustainability*, 2006, **159**, Issue 1.

> Scopes J. P. London 2012: a new approach to CDM coordination, *Civil Engineering*, 2009, **162**, Issue 2.

> Shin J. H. and Lee I. K. Cheong Gye Cheon restoration in Seoul, Korea, *Civil Engineering*, 2006, **159**, Issue 4.

> Sohail M. and Baldwin A. Partnering with community – an option for infrastructure procurement, *Municipal Engineer*, 2001, **145**, Issue 4.

7.Keeping everything on track

Contents

> *'It is critical to get KPIs aligned with strategic corporate objectives.'* Steve Rowsell, CrossRail

Managing performance

Performance management is a systematic approach to help manage and lead the delivery of projects, linking business goals developed in the planning and development stages to overall project outcomes in the implementation, operation and decommissioning stages (ref Kaplan, 1996; HM Treasury, 2001; Office of Government Commerce, 2007, Building Research Establishment, 2009; Constructing Excellence, 2009; National Audit Office, 2009).

The approach ensures that project success is clearly defined, is measurable and is ultimately achieved. Leaders in client organisations should be personally involved in establishing the system, typically during the development stage, and remain actively involved throughout all subsequent stages of a project's lifecycle.

An effective performance management system has two critical roles to play (see Figure 7.1). First, it is used to translate the strategic intent into clear and meaningful terms to assist clients communicate the strategy to everyone involved in a project. This could be said to be making sure everyone will be 'doing the right things'.

While it is crucial during the early development stage of a project to achieve wide understanding, commitment and motivation, performance management should also be continued throughout all subsequent stages to keep everyone familiar with changes that emerge from ongoing strategic and operational reviews.

Second, an effective performance management system provides feedback about progress being achieved towards the business goals. This flow of information enables client decision makers continually to develop the project programme, based on facts and data, to ensure its success. It also enables the original strategic assumptions within the business case to be tested and adjusted in the light of emerging issues. This could be said to be making sure everyone is 'doing things right'.

Sharing results

Effective internal and external communications about performance and its benefits are vital to the successful delivery of a project. This builds commitment, motivation and confidence among all people involved. The performance management system is an important means to assist with this by providing sound information and data.

Clients should use a wide variety of communication channels to get information out to people. While protecting sensitive financial information, clients should consider distributing their performance-management information on their internet and intranet sites for real-time access by various levels of management, teams and individuals. They could also use periodic reports, newsletters, electronic broadcasts and other visual media to set out their objectives and achievements.

Some of the issues which should be considered are:

> how is communication with the outside world to be handled? Does the project need an external identity and profile? How is communication with the press and media to be handled?

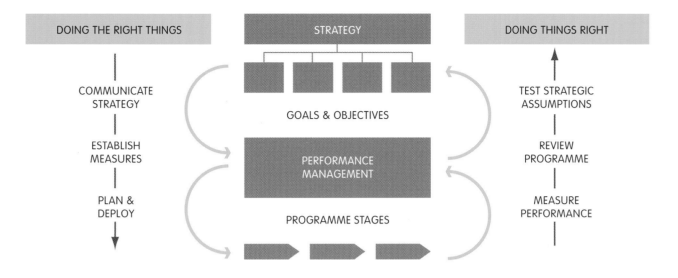

DOING THE RIGHT THINGS

STRATEGY

DOING THINGS RIGHT

COMMUNICATE STRATEGY

TEST STRATEGIC ASSUMPTIONS

GOALS & OBJECTIVES

ESTABLISH MEASURES

PERFORMANCE MANAGEMENT

REVIEW PROGRAMME

PLAN & DEPLOY

PROGRAMME STAGES

MEASURE PERFORMANCE

Figure 7.1. Two critical roles of a performance management system – doing the right things and doing things right

> contracts should have a pre-agreed media communication strategy with staff trained to deal with this.

> are team members allowed to publicise and gain reputational benefit from their involvement with the project?

> *'The clarity of the business plan was crucial; everything was clear and regularly communicated.'*
> Steve Jones, Skanska (Hong Kong Airport)

Accountability for results

The performance management system should be used to set out accountabilities for results that should be clearly assigned and well-understood. To be effective, accountabilities should be agreed formally and signed off by all parties involved in their development to avoid misunderstandings and disappointment. To have any effective meaning at all, accountabilities should be associated with both positive and negative consequences but should not be punitive.

Performance management should be positive and proactive, and not be the basis to apportion blame. Individual culpability is only considered as part of a systems-wide analysis and even then the focus should remain on learning and development. Clients should focus performance management on improving the organisation and its systems, using targets and rewards to motivate people, teams and organisations involved in the programme.

Peoples' behaviours are driven by the consequences of their actions so clients should develop a fair, balanced and motivational environment in terms of compensation, rewards and recognition. It is one of the most powerful levers senior managers have to influence positive programme outcomes because of its effect on behaviours. Clients should not underestimate the profound effect that this can have on overall performance.

> *'It is always positive to work with a performance management system, and it absolutely does affect behaviours.'* Hugh Coakley, Parsons Brinkerhoff

Measurement framework

Key performance indicators (KPIs) are commonly used on successful projects. Clients define these up front and include them within supply contracts in a consistent manner, so that progress can be similarly reviewed across different packages.

KPIs that are normalised are particularly powerful in providing a quick overview for both the client and supply teams. Examples include:

> CPI (cost performance indicator) = budgeted cost of work performed/actual cost of work performed.

> SPI (schedule performance indicator) = budgeted cost of work performed/budgeted cost of work scheduled.

In each case a value greater than 1 is good news and a value less than 1 means that some attention is needed.

However, clients should consider using a balanced set of performance measures, commonly referred to as a 'balanced scorecard' approach. By focusing on prime project outcomes as well as on what influences these outcomes – such as operational effectiveness, and development and learning – clients can build a more comprehensive view of their programmes, which in turn helps them act in the best long-term interests of all parties.

Performance measurement should provide actionable information to decision makers, who should be presented with the results of comprehensive analysis carried out by appropriate subject experts. The analysis should look for deviations from expectations and try to account for these, assess opportunities and risks, forecast future performance and make informed recommendations for change. Measurement becomes counter-productive if used to assign blame or simply to accumulate data and adhere with reporting requirements. The system should allow for control to be cascaded and managed at the lowest effective level.

It is considered that clients should take particular care to ensure that supplier organisations are capable of collecting and providing reliable data for measurement.

Raising performance standards

Benchmarking should be used to establish performance targets as part of a continuous improvement process to ensure that a project remains at the forefront of best practice, continually raising performance expectations. By systematically comparing key features of the project against leading organisations internally and externally, from across the sector and wherever best practice is found, clients can exploit opportunities for improvement and innovation for the overall benefit of the project.

Clients should use targets to set challenging but achievable objectives throughout a project, and should be developed and continuously reviewed on an informed basis taking account of factors such as:

> past performance – baseline data

> competitive and best-practice benchmarks, within the industry sector and beyond

> stakeholder expectations

> programme strategic and operational needs, including future expectations

> senior management and leadership ambitions for the project.

It is considered that 'hard to achieve' goals, objectives and targets are strongly associated with increases in performance.

Performance review

Clients should systematically review programme performance at strategic and operational levels on a regular planned basis. This is considered to be the most important routine activity that project managers and leaders undertake to secure the ongoing capability of their project throughout its various lifecycle stages.

To ensure the performance management system continues to provide relevant and timely information, clients should continually assess whether their current measures are sufficient or excessive, are proving to be useful in leading and managing a project, and are driving towards the desired results.

Targets should also be reviewed regularly, although too-frequent changes in both measures and targets can cause confusion and affect accountabilities and motivation. Changes should be introduced systematically, progressively and with wide communication about the reasons for change.

Summary

> Clients should use performance management systems to communicate the strategic intent and progress achieved towards business goals to everyone involved. They should use the system to assign accountabilities and delegate decision making. It also provides a basis for compensating, rewarding and recognising individual and team performance while encouraging the right behaviours for success.

> A balanced-scorecard approach ensures that the focus is on performance outcomes as well as on what influences these outcomes. Benchmarking is used to establish targets as part of a continuous drive to raise performance standards.

> Project performance should be systematically reviewed at strategic and operational levels on a regular planned basis as this is considered to be the most important routine activity that clients undertake to secure the ongoing capability of their project throughout its various lifecycle stages – planning, development, implementation, operation and decommissioning.

References

1. Building Research Establishment. Key Performance Indicators for the Construction Industry, 2009. www.bre.co.uk/page.jsp?id=1478

2. Constructing Excellence. KPIzone, 2009. www.kpizone.com

3. HM Treasury. Choosing the Right Fabric – A Framework for Performance Information, March 2001. archive.treasury.gov.uk/performance_info/fabric.pdf

4. National Audit Office, Guidance on Performance Measurement, 2009. www.nao.gov.uk/guidance/index.htm

5. Office of Government Commerce. Achieving Excellence in Construction Procurement, Guide 8 – Improving Performance, 2007. www.ogc.gov.uk/ppm_documents_construction.asp

6. Robert S. and Kaplan D. P. Norton. Balanced Scorecard: Translating Strategy into Action, 1996.

8. Taking responsibility for the end result

Contents

> *'Great projects are ones that capture the imagination and bring delight and technical elegance. Ones that are delivered to the lowest common denominator may deliver the required utility but are unlikely to be ranked in the category of 'great'.*
> Ian Gardner, Arup, Client consultant

Post-completion and legacy objectives

The completeness and effectiveness of a project is as much about its performance in operation as it is about its performance in the implementation stage. Clients have a need and a responsibility to consider and define what is expected for the post-construction activities of commissioning, operation and maintenance. Increasingly there is also a need to consider and define approaches to legacy and decommissioning.

Clients should consider the following issues:

> continuity between a project's lifecycle stages of implementation, operation and eventual decommissioning

> specifications for safe operation and maintenance

> allocation between capital expenditure and operational expenditure in the context of design life and allocation of responsibilities

> future proofing such as designing for in-service upgrades or future expansion

> aspirations for legacy value, design life and sustainability

> planning for decommissioning.

> *'Plan to finish the job the day you start it.'*
> Mike Glover, Arup, Lead consultant

Planning ahead

Construction projects are generally 'enabling'; whether through construction of a building that will provide user facilities, or of infrastructure that will help enable society to function. It can be argued that nothing is of greater legacy value to society than investment today in good infrastructure for the benefit of future generations.

Therefore, how a project is received will ultimately be judged by the users, or society at large, and the values they attribute to it. Clearly cost and programme matter, and need to be responsibly managed against targets, but the success of a project will, in the long term, be judged for its quality and performance in use (ref Saxon, 2005; Office of Government Commerce, 2007a; Construction Clients' Group, 2008a).

Clients thus need to plan ahead for performance in use and to be clear of the aspirations for legacy value. For example, the project may be adopting technologies and operating criteria that are a step-change from the experience and expertise of existing operations and maintenance teams, who may need retraining and involvement throughout the project.

Operating and maintenance instructions, together with acceptance records, as-built records and lists of defects, are normally requirements of the construction contracts. Sometimes this is extended to reliability, availability, maintainability and safety/serviceability ('RAMS') databases that are required to be compiled by the construction team. However, if there is not an agreed body with a responsibility to receive, take ownership and understand how to access these often complex documents, there can be a disconnection between seller and buyer.

The best time competitively to buy maintenance agreements is when suppliers are bidding for installation work. To negotiate with them afterwards leaves clients in a much weaker position. A further consideration is that a supplier who has already been committed to a maintenance contract (or at least the client holding the option of one) is likely to put more care and attention into getting the quality of the original installation work right. There will be a vested interest in achieving good quality and high performance if this reduces its future maintenance costs.

The time needed properly to commission and hand-over a complex project can be considerable, and needs to be fully integrated within the project programme from the outset. Equally, the consequences of phased handovers or the need for separate client or concessionaire fit-out activities need to be planned for.

In many modern infrastructure projects it is not just the physical construction but the customer interfaces, public facilities and information systems that need to be in place for a project to be fully operational. These need to be planned as an integral part of the project programme.

Defining operating requirements

Experienced clients know that if specified facilities are constructed and properly commissioned then they will be able to implement and achieve their operating requirements. In such cases, clients effectively take responsibility for the performance in use, so the responsibilities of the supply team effectively end with the start of operation.

In other cases, clients may take a different approach. They may know the minimum operational performance that will satisfy their business case, but be open-minded or not know how to define the facilities to deliver this. In such cases, clients can set a performance requirement and require the supply team to determine the specification and execute the work to meet this required performance.

The two approaches are fundamentally different and can influence the approach to a project, its procurement and the means by which suppliers receive payment. Traditional construction contracts awarded following a design process based on a predetermined client brief tend to suit the first approach. Design-build-finance-operate contracts tend to be more aligned with the second approach.

Another thing clients need to consider is, 'what you measure is what you get'. If a project sets fairly general requirements for performance, then clients have the opportunity to apply this generally in judging the achieved results. By comparison, if clients have prepared a very detailed specification to outline exactly what is required, then they cannot be critical of the supply team if the result does not meet some other unspecified criteria or undefined expectation.

The above points can be applied to the whole project or to specific component parts of it.

'While it is, of course, the client that will have to take the final decision on any aspect relating to project or programme strategy, the client will benefit from taking on board advice from external stakeholders in developing this vision. The client may not be able to appreciate issues related to the delivery or end use of a building or structure that will be more obvious to those that have to construct or use them.' Project manager

Preparing for obsolescence

The business case for a project will establish the timeframe for the investment and return on this. The level of specification and quality of a project can then be matched to suit this to optimise return on investment and to achieve the right balance between capital and operational expenditure. If the plan is for a clear handover from the implementation team to an operating team, then the interface between capital and operational expenditure needs to be unambiguously defined. This is less critical when the same organisation is responsible for both.

Different components of a project will have different life expectancies, so care is needed when talking about 'design life'. A project may have a 120-year design life to match with the overall business case. However, it is clearly impossible and unnecessary for every single component to be designed and specified to last for 120 years. Clients should thus consider defining what is meant by project design life, the influence of planned maintenance on functionality in use and the need for some redundancy or over-capacity to enable outages.

A further factor may be the cost and effort involved in allowing for future flexibility or adaptability to be able to modify the utilisation and thus avoid obsolescence. In general, designed-in flexibility can be expensive as it is seldom possible to fully anticipate future requirements and to include for these up front. Often the ability to adapt is more useful and less expensive in terms of up-front investment.

Decommissioning

One of the great challenges in a sustainable environment is that projects should have no long-term detrimental impact. Clients clearly have a prime responsibility for this. Their business case and Client Brief for projects should therefore include not only the cost of building and operating the project but also some consideration of safe and environmentally responsible decommissioning. Materials should be specified and designed to satisfy these whole-project objectives.

Experience shows that most materials can be recycled or reprocessed once separated out. Some can be crushed or reused without major treatment and are reasonably inert, while others need specialist reprocessing that can only be achieved once transported to suitable facilities. Therefore, increasingly, it is the ability to sort and separate materials effectively that most influences decommissioning.

Designs should also take advantage of recycled materials from previous decommissioned projects and in turn facilitate future recycling.

'We should not leave the planet in a worse condition than we inherited it in.' Client Consultant

Legacy and sustainability

It is important to deliver projects that have clearly defined legacy values and which have strong sustainability credentials (ref Office of Government Commerce, 2007b; Construction Clients' Group, 2008b; HM Government and Strategic Forum for Construction, 2008). While there is much talk of sustainability, the degree to which this can be measured to know what has been achieved is often less easy to gauge.

The sustainability agenda offers an opportunity for clients to demonstrate leadership. For example, it is often more expensive to use sustainably sourced materials so, if the supply chain's driver is commercial, sustainability and best value will be lost in a race to the lowest price. But by considering whole-life costing, and looking at sustainability in both construction and operation, choices in design and construction can improve the long-term sustainability of a project. There are many definitions of sustainability. A widely used and internationally accepted definition of sustainable development is 'development that meets the needs of the present without compromising the ability of future generations to meet their own needs' (ref Brundtland, 1987).

Sustainable development is often characterised as having three dimensions: environmental, social and economic. It is when these three dimensions come together that a project can be considered to be sustainable. This is symbolised in Figure 8.1.

When these three aspects of a project combine to make a sustainable project it is sometimes defined as meeting the 'triple bottom line'.

Clients should consider whole-life costing to improve the long-term sustainability of a project. They should consider sustainable options during the planning and development stages, as innovations and new technologies are best considered by an integrated team when defining specifications.

Energy costs and recycling have been made more prominent by increases in the price of fossil fuels. This emphasis has initiated a focus within construction on reducing energy costs and increased recycling. Travel is also a key issue for project sustainability. Video conferencing has an invaluable place, but clients should recognise that relationships need to be started and nurtured by face-to-face meetings, with video conferencing being used once the relationship has developed.

Clients should also consider the carbon emissions that will be generated by their project. Many are considering the impacts their projects will have on climate change and setting carbon targets for the project.

Clients should consider measuring the legacy and sustainability outcomes of their projects and position them relative with other projects. As mentioned in previous chapters, there are national and international recognised standards for registering and gaining certification for aspects of sustainability performance, such as

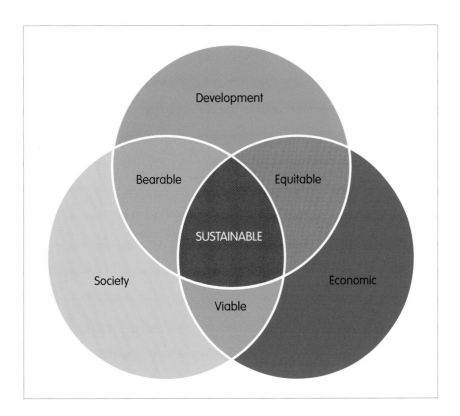

Figure 8.1. The three dimensions of sustainable development

CEEQUAL, LEED and BREEAM (ref US Green Building Council, 1008; BRE Global Ltd, 2009; CEEQUAL, 2009). The decision to seek such certification needs to be taken early and the standard sought to be established at the outset together with the level of attainment – for example, silver, gold, platinum – within this standard.

Like quality and environmental standards, there is often a need for a degree of independent audit and monitoring associated with sustainability certification. It may therefore be appropriate for clients to appoint specialists at an early stage to advise on this and to set up sustainability objectives and monitoring.

Case study – use of renewable energy sources in school design

At the new Langley Park School in Bromley, a very early focus on achieving a renewable energy outcome has resulted in lower overall lifecycle energy costs, a 20% reduction in energy costs and a 60% reduction in overall carbon footprint. Technology included biomass boiler, photovoltaics and a small combined-heat-and-power plant.

Summary

> Clients have a need and a responsibility to consider and define what is expected for the post-construction activities of commissioning, operation and maintenance of their projects. Increasingly there is also a need to consider and define approaches to legacy, sustainability and decommissioning.

> Clients need to take care how they define the operating requirements for their projects, using either a physical or performance specification as appropriate. They need to understand the concept of design life as it relates to each part of a project, and consider allowing for future flexibility and decommissioning.

> Whole-life costs, including maintenance, energy usage and travel, need to be considered in the overall business case for a project. A comprehensive information database on a project should also be maintained from inception through to final decommissioning.

References

1. BRE Global Ltd. *BRE Environmental Assessment Method*, 2009. www.breeam.org/

2. Brundtland G.H. *Our Common Future, Report of the World Commission on Environment and Development*, World Commission on Environment and Development 1987

3. Civil Engineering Environmental Quality Assessment and Award Scheme, 2009. www.ceequal.com/

4. Construction Clients' Group. *Client's Commitments Best Practice Guide*, Chapter 5 Design quality, Constructing Excellence, London, November 2008a. www.constructingexcellence.org.uk/sectorforums/constructionclientsgroup/clientcommitments/5.%20DQ.pdf

5. Construction Clients' Group. *Client's Commitments Best Practice Guide*, Chapter 4 Sustainability, Constructing Excellence, London, November 2008b. www.constructingexcellence.org.uk/sectorforums/constructionclientsgroup/clientcommitments/4.%20Sust.pdf

6. HM Government and Strategic Forum for Construction. *Strategy for Sustainable Construction*, Department for Business, Enterprise and Regulatory Reform, London, June 2008. www.berr.gov.uk/files/file46535.pdf

7. Office of Government Commerce, Design Quality, CP0069, OGC, London, 2007a. www.ogc.gov.uk/documents/CP0069AEGuide9.pdf

8. Office of Government Commerce. Sustainability, CP0016, OGC, London, 2007b. www.ogc.gov.uk/documents/CP0016AEGuide11.pdf

9. Saxon R. Be Valuable: A Guide to Creating Value in the Built Environment, Constructing Excellence, London, November 2005. www.saxoncbe.com/bevaluable.pdf

10. US Green Building Council, Leed, 2008. www.usgbc.org/DisplayPage.aspx?CategoryID=19

Further reading

> Adetunji, Price, Fleming. Achieving sustainability in the construction supply chain, *Engineering Sustainability*, 01/09/2008.

> Dempsey. Does quality of the built environment affect social cohesion? *Urban Design and Planning*, 01/09/2008.

Appendix:
ClientMAP –
the client best
practice online
assessment tool

The client best practice guide's online maturity assessment profile tool, ClientMAP, is freely available through the Institution of Civil Engineers website. ClientMAP has been developed to help clients assess their readiness and ongoing capability to lead construction projects in relation to the best practices identified in this guide.

ClientMAP is a self assessment questionnaire that will help users challenge their own thinking and guide activities within the project to help maximise their effectiveness. Whilst it is based entirely around best practice guidance found in the guide, tools of this type do not replace the personal experience necessary to deliver major projects and nor are they a substitute for seeking sound advice from professionals. However, a ClientMAP assessment will compliment these activities by providing a consistent and structured appraisal of capabilities. These can be monitored over time and between projects contributing to increased effectiveness and ultimately to more certainty about project success.

The assessment is divided into three sections, each covering a number of chapters in the guide – as shown in the following table.

ClientMAP can be used at any stage in the project's lifecycle. At the start of a project it can test a client's intentions and plans, and once underway it can be used to assess the reality of the developing situation in the project and provide guidance on opportunities to improve.

The benefits of using ClientMAP are:

> rapid and accessible self-assessment of a client's readiness and ongoing capability to lead projects in relation to best-practices, setting the project up for success

> structured and consistent analysis of client capabilities that can be monitored for improvements over time and between projects, enabling benchmarking against the best

> ready identification of strengths and opportunities for improvement that can be incorporated into project development plans, driving continuous improvement.

Chapter	Assessment tool sections
1. What makes a successful client?	Setting up for success
2. Essential stages of a project	
3. Developing a delivery strategy	
4. Establishing the client team	
5. Procuring the supply team	Integrating the teams
6. Caring for people and the environment	
7. Keeping everything on track	Driving for results and outcomes
8. Taking responsibility for the end result	

Users will be aware that self assessments tend to introduce a degree of optimism and bias. To overcome this tendency when answering questions it is best to focus on specific situations within the project and consider tangible evidence wherever this is available. Independent assessments from competent providers may be used to provide a balanced view and address this risk from time to time.

The ClientMAP self assessment report characterises client capability against a scale of five levels of maturity, consistent with leading methods commonly used by the OGC, Constructing Excellence and other business development groups. Maturity levels are typically as shown in the diagram below:

The report provides an overall 'maturity score', as well as a maturity score for each of the three broad aspects discussed above, to help refine and focus user's development plans. A

further level of feedback is provided in the report describing 'areas of strength' and 'opportunities for improvement' based on the pattern of answers to the detailed questions within the questionnaire.

Ultimately ClientMAP will be developed to include benchmarking data to allow users to characterise their capability against sector norms, but in the meantime a database of user responses will be built up to lead towards this goal.

In conclusion, the authors of this client guide wish to strongly recommend that readers use the online self assessment tool to help develop their capability in leading, integrating and driving project teams to success.

ClientMAP can be accessed directly from the ICE website at: www.ice.org.uk/ClientMAP

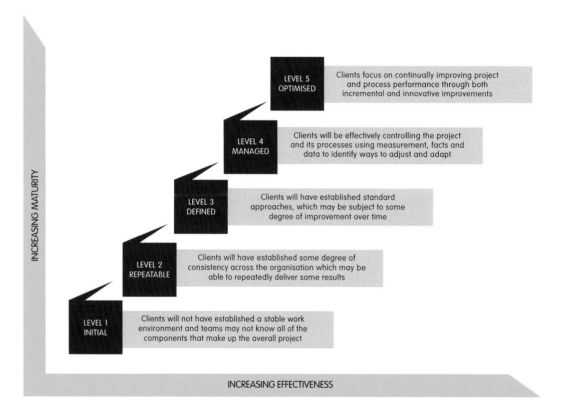

Client capability – the five levels of client maturity

Index